Frederick Locker

Patchwork

Frederick Locker

Patchwork

ISBN/EAN: 9783337977290

Printed in Europe, USA, Canada, Australia, Japan

Cover: Foto ©Thomas Meinert / pixelio.de

More available books at **www.hansebooks.com**

FREDERICK LOCKER

LONDON

SMITH, ELDER, & CO., 15 WATERLOO PLACE

1879

DEDICATION.

While arranging this little book, I have once more enjoyed the society of a few friends and of many pleasant companions, dead and living, and it would have pleased me to have dedicated it to more than one of them.

I have a friend who is still with us, and whose name I should have well liked to have seen on this page, but is he not a distinguished dignitary of our National Church? and could I have asked him to take so incongruous a collection of trifles under his decanal wings?

If I had asked him, he might not have denied me.

I think I will dedicate my collection to my friends yet living, and to the memory of those who are gone.

FREDERICK LOCKER.

25 CHESHAM STREET, S.W.: 1878.

PREFACE.

I DO not know whether a reference to Dr. Johnson's Dictionary would show that a Commonplace-book is a book kept by a commonplace sort of person, but I should not be surprised if the Doctor had thought so, and, certainly, there is a very general opinion that collections of such scraps are mighty poor reading : in sustained and coherent interest not a whit better than the Doctor's own lexicon.

Such volumes are generally a miscellaneous gathering of fragments, which the editor fancies, in a vague sort of way, will be amusing or edifying to the general public. Now as my detached pieces were brought together with no idea of pleasing anybody but myself, I hope they will have a more individual flavour, and so, in some measure, escape this very serious charge.

I fear that I may annoy some readers, for, though I have taken pains, no doubt I have sorely mal-treated many of the extracts, picked up, as they were, from all sorts of people, in all kinds of places, from the corners of newspapers, and such like.

For instance, I remember hearing one of the stories—one of the very best of them, mind—in a Turkish bath ; it was related by a personage with whom I was not acquainted, I could not even see him, and, as, like our first parents in Paradise, I had neither pencil nor paper about me, I was not able to secure chapter and verse.

Dear Reader, if you find your pet story has been especially massacred, make up your benevolent mind that it was the very story (which there is no doubt at all it was !) which I picked up in the Turkish bath.

I have often refrained from citing authorities, either because I did not know them, or for fear of ascribing wrongly, and thus giving just cause of offence to my accomplished friend the author of 'Pearls and Mock Pearls of History.' By this, and by other sins of omission I fear I have often defrauded authors of their just dues. I repeat that when I penned these paragraphs and made these extracts I had no notion of printing them, or I should have taken more care in their transcription, and I should certainly have been a little less vernacular in my style, which is, I own, occasionally unworthy of the dignity of print—but I feared that if I re-wrote them they might lose any little freshness they possess.

F. L.

PATCHWORK.

WANT OF EARNESTNESS.

ISAAC BARROW (1630–1677) could not tolerate people who looked on life merely from the grotesque or ludicrous point of view. 'If it is true,' said he, 'that nothing has for you any relish except painted comfits and unmeaning trifles, that not even wisdom will please you, unless without its own peculiar flavour, nor truth, unless seasoned with a jest, nor reason, unless cloaked in fun, then in an unlucky hour have I been assigned as your purveyor, neither born nor bred a such a frivolous confectionery. The insatiable appetite for laughter keeps itself within no bounds. Have you crowded to this place for the purpose of listening, and studying, and making progress, or only for the sake of laughing at this thing, and making a jest of that other? There is nothing so remote from levity which you do not instantly transmute into mirth and absurdity, and let a discourse be such as to move no laughter, nothing else will please, neither dignity, nor gravity, nor solidity, neither strength, nor point, nor polish.'

B

PETS.

Human nature is not thoroughly base, it must have
something to cling to ; for instance, a husband or
wife, a father or a mother, a son or a daughter—if
can't have these, it puts up with an uncle or even
grandmother.   The same with *la belle passion*, but
will not enter on that now, it is too suggestive, an
would take far too long.   And it is the same wi
friendship.   Some people are entirely dependent
their friendships, they cling to the beloved as iv
embraces the oak, and they do not look unlovely a
they so cling.   I believe those who have this capacit
are not the less happy for it.   Life runs very pleasant
for them, their hours dance away with down upo
their feet !   There are others, again, who are much
more independent, if they cannot find a human bein
handy, they put up with a pug or a cockatoo.   I kno
one or two very worthy people who find old chin
monsters, or even a rare postage-stamp, all-sufficin
but I think I have never come across any one wh
was entirely self-contained.

I have a friend who is blessed with a charmin
wife and very fine children—he is a model husban
and father, but his heart is so capacious that he ha
also found accommodation for a huge brute of
Patagonian poodle, and this too in a not by any means
capacious establishment.   The animal came to him

from that country as a puppy, and it increased in
weight and size at such a bewildering rate that it
almost took his poor wife's breath away. She hopes
'Fang' has at last done growing. The enormous
beast, who under that murderous name makes the
earth to quake beneath him, and the population to
tremble before him, is supremely good-natured, but, I
suspect, he is out-of-the-common stupid, and he is
useless too, for, as you may suppose, he is nothing of a
mouser. The house is a fair size,

> But if it's entered by a rat
> There is no room to bring a cat.

'Fang' completely fills every chamber! and he empties
it, too; for does not one whisk of his tail make hay
with those little occasional tables, and the *objets d'art*
that cover them? those tables which are so much in
the way, and which might well be called traps to catch
unwary visitors. It would be interesting to see the
statistics of Fang's butcher's account.

His gracious mistress (it would seem a mockery to
call anybody his master) is not fanciful, but 'Fang' is
so monstrous, and has such a threatening black jowl,
that if any one of the children is out of sight longer
than usual, she cannot get rid of the idea that perhaps
'Fang' has swallowed it. My friend is not a giant,
and therefore, as he and his pet are inseparable, if I
should ever chance to meet the dog without his
master (it is impossible I could ever meet the master

without the dog) I should feel sure that the dog had
made one gulp of him. It is diverting to see my
friend return from a walk, and squeeze back into his
house, for the hall will not hold him and his pet at
the same moment.

Fang's master (I believe he is known in the
neighbourhood as Fang's slave) lives within an easy
walk of the metropolis, and he delights in the humours
of the capital, and the grateful capital simply adores
him, but we never see him now! Poor fellow, he is
such a slave to his pet that he is afraid to leave him
at home, he cannot *shunt* him, and he dares not take
him with him to London. We never see our poor
friend now. See how disastrous it is to have *bow-
wow* on the brain!

The following story of a pet is not to be read by
anybody who is more than twelve years old :—

I have another pair of friends. They possess a
delightful pet—a tame rook. He quits his own kind,
by *preference*, to visit these fascinating but feather-
less bipeds. I happened to be staying with them in
Cheshire. The hour was very early morning. There
was a tap-tap at my window—what could it portend?
Like the adorer of *la belle qui fût Heaulmière*, I
have tapped at other people's casements before now.
I know the sound, in fact, and appreciate the situation.
I listened consciously and I opened the lattice coyly,
and I was on the point of peeping out, when in

flapped the rook, and in a perfectly well-bred manner immediately made himself at home with my soap-dish. His visit at an end, out he hopped again, and proceeded to call on one or two other friends ; and, at breakfast, we were able to compare notes about him, and bear testimony to his discreet behaviour.

The same evening I saw him in the lofty elm-trees, flopping about and cawing with his natural nest-fellows, who, ' deliberate birds and prudent all,' were tearing each other's habitats to pieces.

I must now tell you how it was that my friends first made the rook's friendship. It would appear that at a very early age he was kicked out of ' the family tree,' and broke his leg. My benevolent friends succoured him, made much of him, and, when he was strong enough to fly, he, for a time, returned to his wild life, but he did not forget them, he often came back, and paid them a more than flying visit. He also made friends with the parrot, which although a cynical fowl, afterwards did him a good turn, and in this wise. One day, while he and the parrot were on the lawn together, a bird of prey suddenly swooped down, · and without doubt, if it had not been for poor Polly, would have carried him off, there and then. But, as it happened, the parrot set up an unearthly *screech-screech,* whereupon the kite dropped his victim and vanished. Since that day the bond between my friends, and the parrot, and the rook, has been continually drawn closer.

The rook, though still a worshipper of nature, is now their *daily* visitor.

He has always been accounted a moral bird, who never did anything to discredit his clerical. garb, but he has his weaknesses, and for instance—a young lady was staying in the house who was warmly attached to him, and, one day, on the lawn, she gave him her ring to play with, he accepted it in his beak, gave a hop and a wriggle, and off he flew with it. It was a most valuable diamond ring and yet this delightful young person was as cheerful as possible under her loss, she was rather amused about it than otherwise. She was interested in the rook, and really it looked as if he was going to be married. She was rewarded for her good nature, for the impudent fellow soon brought back the ring, and next morning, when he tapped at her casement, and carried in with him a delicious perfume of the morning roses and the newly-mown hay, he paid her a much longer visit than usual. So much for pets.

AN ENVIABLE GIFT.

Richard Crashaw sent George Herbert's book of sacred poems intituled 'The Temple,' to a gentle-woman, with the following lines :

> Know you, Fair, on what you look?
> Divinest love lies in this book,

Expecting fire from your eyes
To kindle this his sacrifice.
When your hands untie these strings,
Think you've an Angel by the wings—
ne that gladly would be nigh
o wait upon each morning sigh,
o flutter in the balmy air
Of your well-perfumëd prayer.
These white plumes of his he'll lend you,
Which every day to Heaven will send you,
To take acquaintance of the sphere,
And all the smooth-faced kindred there!
  And tho' Herbert's name do owe
These devotions, Fairest, know
That while *I* lay them on the shrine
Of your white hand, they are *mine*.

BLACK BLOOD.

A lady of my acquaintance, a brunette, happened
to show her maid one of those little sticking-plaster
profiles which they used to call *Silhouettes*. It was the
portrait of the lady's aunt, whom the girl had never
seen; and she said quite innocently, 'La, ma'am, I
always thought as how you had some black relations,
you are so dark-like yourself, you know.'

THE BIBLE.

'What is there (in that romantic interest, and patriarchal simplicity, which goes to the heart of a people) equal to the story of Joseph and his brethren, of Rachel and Laban, of Jacob's dream, of Ruth and Boaz, the descriptions in the book of Job, the deliverance of the Jews out of Egypt, or the account of their captivity and return from Babylon? There is in all these parts of the Scripture, and numberless more of the same kind, to pass over the Orphic hymns of David, the prophetic denunciations of Isaiah, or the gorgeous visions of Ezekiel, an originality, a vastness of conception, a depth and tenderness of feeling, and a touching simplicity in the mode of narration, which he who does not feel need be made of no penetrable stuff.

'There is something in the character of Christ, too (leaving religious faith quite out of the question), of more sweetness and majesty, and more likely to work a change in the mind of man, by the contemplation of its idea alone, than any to be found in history whether actual or feigned. This character is that of a sublimed humanity, such as was never seen on earth before or since. This shone manifestly both in His words and actions, we see it in His washing the disciples' feet the night before His death, that unspeakable instance of humility and love, above all art, all meanness, and all pride, and in the leave He took of them on that occasion,

" My peace I give unto you ; that peace which the world cannot give, give I unto you," and in His last commandment that they should " love one another." Who can read the account of His behaviour on the cross, when turned to His mother He said "Woman, behold thy son, and to the disciple John, " Behold thy mother,", and "from that hour that disciple took her to his own home," without having his heart smote within him ! We see it in His treatment of the woman taken in adultery ; His religion was the religion of the heart. We see it in His discourses with His disciples, as they walked together towards Emmaus, when their hearts burned within them; in His Sermon from the Mount, in His parable of the Good Samaritan, and in that of the Prodigal Son. In every act and word of His life a grace, a mildness, a dignity and love, a patience and wisdom worthy of the Son of God. His whole life and being were imbued, steeped in this word *Charity.*

' It was the spring, the well-head from which every thought and feeling gushed into act, and it was this that breathed a mild glory from His face in that last agony on the cross, "when the meek Saviour bowed His head and died," praying for His enemies.

' He was the first true teacher of morality, for He alone conceived the idea of a pure humanity. He redeemed man from the worship of that idol self, and instructed him by precept and example to love his neighbour as himself, to forgive his enemies, to do good to those that curse us and despitefully use us, He taught the love of good for the sake of good, without regard to personal or sinister views, and made the affections of the heart the sole seat of morality, instead of the pride of the understanding, or the stern s of the will. In answering the question " Who is our neigh-bour?" as one who stands in need of our assistance, and whose wounds we can bind up, He has done more to humanize the thoughts and tame the unruly passions than all who have tried to reform and benefit man-kind.'

William Hazlitt.

> "'Tis very vain for me to boast,
> How small a price my Bible cost;
> The Day of Judgment will make clear
> 'Twas very cheap, or very dear.'

Michael Scott.

ALMOST TOO CEREMONIOUS.

A gentleman walked up to another gentleman, who was standing before the fire in a Coffee Room, and immediately said, 'I beg your pardon, Sir, but may I ask your name?' 'I am not in the habit, Sir,' said the other man, 'of giving my name to strangers, but, as you are so pertinacious, Sir, my name is Thompson, Sir.' 'Then, Mr. Thompson, Sir,' said the first speaker, 'now I know your name, I beg, Sir, to inform you that your coat tails are on fire.'

PATRIOTISM.

, It is recorded of Dr. W. P. Alison, the celebrated physician, who died in 1859, that, as a child, he had spoken to a man, who had spoken to Henry Jenkins, who lived to the age of 169, and had, when a boy, carried arrows to the English archers, who won the battle of Flodden in 1513.

There is a story in Lockhart's ' Life of Scott ' of a blacksmith, whom Scott had known as a horse-doctor, and whom he afterwards found at a small country town south of the border, practising medicine with a reckless use of ' laudamy and calomy.' The man apologised for the mischief he might be doing, by the assurance that, ' at any rate,' it ' would be lang before it made up for Flodden.'

It may be presumed that, if it had been possible, the *ci-devant* blacksmith would not have altogether objected to prescribe for Henry Jenkins ; but, if so, would Jenkins have survived to converse with Alison's informant?

SONNET.

' If thou must love me, let it be for nought
Except for love's sake only. Do not say
" I love her for her smile—her look—her way
Of speaking gently,—for a trick of thought

That falls in well with mine, and certes brought
A sense of pleasant ease on such a day "—
For these things, in themselves, Beloved, may
Be changed, or change for thee,—and love, so
    wrought,
May be unwrought so.   Neither love me for
Thine own dear pity's wiping my cheeks dry,—
A creature might forget to weep, who bore
Thy comfort long, and lose thy love thereby !
But love me for love sake, that evermore
.Thou may'st love on, thro' love's eternity.'

Elizabeth B. Browning.

  .*. This has been said before, but never more
touchingly or eloquently.

EDGAR POE.

  Some one has observed that ' Edgar Poe's muse
by the side of his abominable life ' (I believe it has
been lately ascertained that his life was anything but
abominable, which is unfortunate for this remark) was
like a nunnery in the heart of a disorderly and immoral
city, surrounded, but not contaminated by it.'

  It is a great advantage for a man of literary genius
to have been an unfortunate scamp, and almost as
lucky to have been a worthy simple-minded creature
of *singularly* evil fortunes. How much Cowper has
gained by his craziness, and Goldsmith would have

lost if he had not been so absurd and impecunious !
Then we have Marlowe and Byron. We should never
have heard of Savage had he been a respectable man.

If there were a tradition that Southey had got tipsy,
and had tried to kiss Miss Maria Edgeworth, or that
he had pledged the 'Curse of Kehama' at the pawn-
broker's, perhaps people would think a good deal more
of the 'Curse of Kehama.'

The first flight of virtuous biographers fill in all
the dark shadows, laying them on thick ; then come
a party of wild white-washers, and all the time the
game is kept alive, the Author is talked about, his
works sell, and are perhaps read. This reaction about
is really too hard upon him—if ever his character
d be entirely rehabilitated the world will find out
as something of a literary charlatan.

———◆———

E STYLE AND SPIRIT OF THE CLASSIC
WRITERS.

Let us consider, too, how differently young and
are affected by the words of some classic author,
as Homer or Horace. Passages, which to a boy
but rhetorical commonplaces, neither better nor
e than a hundred others which any clever writer
t supply ; which he gets by heart and thinks very
and imitates, as he thinks, successfully in his own

flowing versification, at length come home to him,
when long years have passed, and he has had experience of life, and pierce him as if he had never
before known them, with their sad earnestness and
vivid exactness.

‘ Then he comes to understand how it is that lines,
the birth of some chance morning or evening at an
Ionian festival or among the Sabine Hills, have lasted
generation after generation, for thousands of years ;
with a power over the mind, and a charm, which the
current literature of his own day, with all its obvious
advantages, is utterly unable to rival.’

‘ Grammar of Assent.’

₊*₊ How transparent is this thought—how s
are the words, and yet the whole seems to tingle
a suppressed emotion !

BEAUMARCHAIS.

Beaumarchais was *blâmé* by the Court, and
effect of that *blâme* was very serious. It made a
legally infamous. But the public feeling was
strongly with Beaumarchais that he paraded
stigma as if it were a mark of honour. He gave
self such airs that somebody said to him, ‘ Monsieu
n'est pas assez que d'être blâmé ; il faut être mode

THE LAMENT FOR CULLODEN.

Burns's beautiful lament for Culloden is composed of two stanzas, in the first the lovely lass of Inverness mourns the loss of her father and her three brothers ; and it is only in the concluding stanza that she .says

> And by them lies the dearest lad
> That ever blest a woman's ee !

Not mentioning the lad in the first stanza makes it much more impressive, and more pathetic when he *is* mentioned.

WITHOUT AND WITHIN.

' My coachman, in the moonlight there,
　Looks thro' the side-light of the door ;
I hear him with his brethren swear,
　As I could do,—but only more.

' Flattening his nose against the pane,
　He envies me my brilliant lot,
Breathes on his frozen fist in vain,
　And dooms me to a place more hot.

' He sees me in to supper go,
　A Silken Wonder by my side,
Bare arms, bare shoulders, and a row
　Of flounces for the door too wide.

'He thinks how happy is my arm,
   'Neath its white-gloved and jewell'd load;
And wishes me some dreadful harm,
   Hearing the merry corks explode.

'Meanwhile I inly curse the bore
   Of hunting still the same old coon,
And envy him, outside the door,
   The golden quiet of the moon.

'The winter wind is not so cold
   As the bright smile he sees me win,
Nor the host's oldest wine so old
   As our poor gabble, sour and thin.

'I envy him the rugged prance
   By which his freezing feet he warms,
And drag my lady's chains, and dance,
   The galley slave of dreary forms.

'O, could he have my share of din,
   And I his quiet! past a doubt
'Twould still be one man bored within,
   And just another—bored without.'

                          J. Russell Lo·

PANACEA FOR SEA-SICKNESS.

Lady —— was crossing in the steamer from Honfleur to Havre, a passage of about one hour, and occasionally rather rough. Among the passengers was a cocky and very absurd little Frenchman. Before they started he had talked a good deal about sea-sickness, and the remedies usually employed—'Quant à moi, quand je suis en mer je ferme les yeux, et je pense à une jolie femme—je pense à Marie Stuart.' Very shortly afterwards his fellow-passengers had proof positive of the utter inadequacy of this vaunted charm.

THE POPE.

ss D., on her return to the Highlands of Scotland, Rome, went to see an auld Scottish wife, and to interest the old woman, 'I have been to Rome saw you—I have seen all sorts of great people ve seen the Pope.' The sympathetic old dame d with animation, 'The Pope of Rome !—Honest !—haze he ony faimly?'

A LOVER'S ATTENTIONS.

Alas, I had not rendered up my heart
Had he not loved me first ; but he preferred me

C

Above the maidens of my age and rank;
Still shunn'd their company, and still sought mine;
I was not won by gifts, but still he gave;
And all his gifts, tho' small, yet spoke his love.
He pick'd the earliest strawberries in woods,
The cluster'd filberds, and the purple grapes:
He taught a prating stare to speak my name;
And when he found a nest of nightingales,
Or callow linnets, he would show 'em me,
And let me take 'em out.'   John Dryden.

.   .   .   .

———◆◇◆———

MR. ROGERS'S POETRY.

I have always been very fond of Mr. Rogers's
called ' A Wish.'   This is the first stanza : -

> Mine be a cot beside a hill;
>   A bee-hive's hum shall soothe my ear;
> A *willowy* brook, that *turns* a mill,
>   With *many* a fall, shall *linger* near.

The words printed in italics are singularly ha
their sound is very suggestive of a winding strea
water; and though the ideas may be commonpl
enough, and the wish could hardly be sincere—
least I should judge so from my recollection of
22 St. James's Place—it is a graceful little poe
and I should think it might survive many mo
pretentious productions.

Rogers never offends against taste, and, if he does not greatly stimulate his reader, at any rate he does not exasperate him. There are poems, and there are pictures, which one would not think half so bad if they were not quite so good. For instance, let us suppose that the artist is a man of vigour, there is a blowsy sentiment about his work, or a bloated power, and it arrests you, you cannot ignore him, and at last you get to hate him.

It is somewhat the same with a face. I know a woman, she is desperately ugly, as ugly as sin, and (I venture to think) almost as agreeable; but she has big, bright eyes, and if it were not for those eyes her :treme plainness might never have arrested me; as is, when I look at her, I am always arrested, and her ;liness makes me gasp again.

he two next anecdotes are taken from Dean say's 'Reminiscences.' It is pleasant to read that and to think that it was compiled by a Scottish . iastic. The Dean was a man of real piety, he ree from cant, a refined and loveable person, and ust have been a bold man to publish such a ction. He has left us a most interesting legacy, Scotland and England should be grateful for the k, and to the man who gave it.

"IT'S NO' MY WIG."

'The Laird of Balnamoon (pronounced *Bonny-moon*), dining out, took a little too much wine, and, returning home, his servant had to drive him over a very wild and desolate tract of country, called Munrimmon Moor. While crossing it, the laird's hat and wig fell off, and the servant got down, picked them up, and brought them to his master. He took the hat, but declined the wig—" It's no' my wig, Hairy, lad ; it's no' *my* wig," and he stoutly refused to have anything to do with it. *Hairy* lost patience, being naturally anxious to get home, and he remonstrated thus with his master : " Ye'd better tak' it, sir, for there's nae waile o' wigs " (choice of perukes) " on Munrimmon Moor." '

A TENDER CONSCIENCE.

Mr. Wilson, the Scottish vocalist, was ta lessons from Mr. Finlay Dunn, who had just retu from Italy, much impressed with the deep sentii of the Italian school. Mr. Dunn regretted that pupil's fine voice was marred by want of express and feeling ; so, one day, he said to him : ' Now, Wilson, just try and fancy that I'm your lady-love, t idol of your soul, and then sing to me as you would sing to her.' Poor Mr. Wilson hesitated and blushed, in doubt how far, in his case, such a personification was altogether justifiable; at last he hesitatingly remonstrated with—'Ay, but, Mr. Dunn, sir, ye for-get I'm a married man!'

THE SCOTTISH LANGUAGE.

A Scot in Canada, who generally spoke favourably of the country of his adoption, could not help making the following exception when he compared it with the land of his birth : ' But, oh, sir, there are nae linties in the wuds.' How touching are the words in his own dialect ! The North American woods, although full of birds of beautiful plumage, have no singing birds.

Dean Ramsay mentions this story mainly to show the picturesqueness and beauty of the old Scottish language ; he would imply that linnet does not convey so much of simple beauty, and of pastoral ideas, as belong to the Scottish word *lintie,* and he says the same for *Auld lang syne,* and maintains it has no equi-valent in English.

THE SEMI-DETACHMENT.

' Good-bye, small house, good-bye,
  Tho' weak in roof and rafter,
I will not tell a lie
  To him who cometh after :
I could not meet a charge of guilt
Were I to say thou wert well built.

' Yet thou art sweet tho' small,
  Yet art thou dear tho' crack'd ;
While fearing thou might'st fall
  Our faith remain'd intact :
And lived superior to our fears
For seven short matrimonial years.

' Good-bye, old house, good-bye,
  I brought my bride to thee,
In thee I taught to fly
  My little nestlings three,
So cannot leave thee, my first nest,
Without a sinking at my breast.

' We soar to other fields,
  To woods and pastures new,
And if the prospect yields
  A happiness as true
We scarce can be so brightly blest
Elsewhere as here, thou ill-built nest !

'Begone! ye groundless fears,
 Ye phantoms of the past,
Why should our future years
 Be gloomier than the last?
Because we take a loftier flight,
Why should they not be still more bright?

'Come, then, whate'er betide,
 . Hid in the future's womb,
I and my seven-years' bride
 Will love our seven-years' home.
Good-bye, thou ill-constructed cot,
We love, but recommend thee not.'

Philip Acton.

———◆◆◆——

PUBLIC WORSHIP.

''The religious sentiment of England is not what
it was. In most churches the language of public
worship is of a kind which can at most be appropriate
to a very small fraction of those who use it. The
customs of society draw within the church men of all
grades of piety and of faith. The selfish, the frivolous,
and the sceptical, the worldly, the indifferent, or at
least men whose convictions are but half-formed,
whose zeal is very languid, and whose religious thoughts
are very few, form the bulk of every congregation, and
they are taught to employ language expressing the
very ecstasy of devotion. The words that pass

mechanically from their lips convey in turn the fervour of a martyr, the self-abasement or the rapture of a saint, a passionate confidence in the reality of unseen things, a passionate longing to pass beyond the veil. The effect of this contrast between the habitual language of devotion, and the habitual dispositions of the devotees, between the energy of religious expression and the languor of religious conviction is, in some respects, extremely deleterious. The sense of truth is dulled, men come to regard it as a natural and scarcely censurable thing to attune their language on the highest of all subjects to a key wholly different from their general feelings and beliefs, and that which ought to be the truest of human occupations becomes in fact the most unreal and the most conventional.'

William E. H. Lecky.

.˙. Doubtless this is an unfortunate condition of things, but I do not see how the standard of worship could be lowered to meet the requirements of the majority of an average congregation. I think it will be agreed on all hands that absolute simplicity and veracity of mind are the prime conditions of all piety, but if liturgic and dogmatic teaching endanger these conditions, surely it is more from a too great dictation of doctrinal belief than from a too fervent cry of personal devotion. It seems to me that to profess before God any doctrine which one doubts or rejects, is a definite act of falsehood; but an aspiration to join the flight of more saintly natures that are leading the way, and to try to join in their ascent, by mingling one's voice with theirs, is, at the worst, a substitution of what we wish to feel, and hope to feel, for that which as yet we do not feel.

Ought we to reduce the fervour of public worship till it sinks to the pitch of the average unawakened soul? Must we protect the people, in proportion as they are dull or indifferent, from contact with any spirit higher than their own? Surely not. In most of us there are two natures, a superficial, and a deeper nature. And experience every day proves that the one thing needful to awaken the deeper nature is the appeal of a profound, and I would add, an impassioned faith, a faith already familiar with its sorrows and its aspirations.

LUTHER.

Luther married Catherine Bora, a nun of good family, left homeless and poor; she was plain in person and mind. 'The first year of married life,' says Luther, 'is an odd business; at meals, where you used to be alone, you are yourself and somebody else; when you wake in the morning there are a pair of tails close to you on the pillow. My Katie used to sit with me when I was at work; she thought she ought

not to be silent, she did not know what to say, so she
would ask me, "Herr Doctor, is not the master of the
ceremonies, in Prussia, the brother of the Margrave?"
She was an odd woman.'

Froude's 'Times of Erasmus and Luther.'

BENVENUTO CELLINI.

Benvenuto Cellini tells us that once when in boy-
hood he saw a Salamander come out of the fire, his
grandfather, forthwith, gave him a sound beating, that
he might the better remember so unique a prodigy.

THEOCRITUS.

'That which distinguishes Theocritus from all
other poets is the inimitable tenderness of his passions, and the natural expression of them in words so
becoming of a pastoral. A simplicity shines through
all he writes; he shows his art and learning by
disguising both. His shepherds never rise above their
country education. Even his Doric dialect has an
incomparable sweetness in his clownishness, like a
fair shepherdess in her country russet, talking in a
Yorkshire tone.'   John Dryden (1631-1701).

STONEHENGE.

'That huge dumb heap, which stands on the
blasted heath, and looks like a group of giants, be-
wildered, not knowing what to do, encumbering the
earth, and turned to stone while in the act of warring
on Heaven.' William Hazlitt.

THE 'ST. PETER MARTYR' BY TITIAN.

'Yet why not describe it as we see it still in our
mind's eye, standing on the floor of the Tuileries,
with none of its brightness impaired, through the long
perspective of waning years? There it stands, and
will for ever stand in our imagination, with the dark
scowling terrific face of the murdered monk looking up
to his assassin, the horror-struck features of the flying
priest, and the skirts of his vest waving in the wind.
The shattered branches of the autumnal trees that
feel the coming gale, with that cold convent spire
rising in the distance amidst the sapphire hills and
golden sky, and overhead are seen the cherubim,
bringing with rosy fingers the crown of martyrdom,
and (such is the feeling of truth, and soul of faith in
the picture) you hear floating near, in dim harmonies,
the pealing anthem and the heavenly choir.'
William Hazlitt.

When I last saw this glorious picture it was also

on the ground, but in the sacristy in SS. Giovanni
e Paolo. It was destroyed by fire in 1867.

———•◇•———

LUDOVICO CARRACCI'S PICTURE OF 'SUSANNA.'

'Our heart thrilled with its beauty, and our eyes
filled with tears. How often have we thought of it
since ! How often spoken of it. There it was still,
the same lovely phantom as ever. . . The young
Jewish beauty had been just surprised in that un-
guarded spot, crouching down in one corner of the
picture, the face turned back with a mingled expression
of terror, shame, and unconquerable sweetness, and
the whole figure shrinking into itself with bewitching
grace and modesty.'   William Hazlitt.

———•◇•———

C. E. VON KLEIST.

Kleist, the Poet, killed at Kunersdorf, laughed
loudly just before he expired, at the recollection of the
very extraordinary grimaces a Cossack, who had been
plundering him, on the field of battle, made over the
prize he had found.

A COMPROMISE.

Judge.—'Your client had better make a compromise, ask her what she will take.'

Counsel.—'My good woman, his Lordship asks what you will take.'

Old woman.—'I'm obliged to his Lordship' (curtsey) as he's so kind (curtsey). ' I'll just take a glass o' warm ale.'

A RHYME OF ONE.

You sleep upon your mother's breast,
                    Your race begun,
A welcome, long a wish'd-for guest,
                    Whose age is One.

A baby-boy, you wonder why
                    You cannot run ;
You try to talk—how hard you try !—
                    You're only One.

Ere long you won't be such a dunce ;
                    You'll eat your bun,
And fly your kite, like folk, who once
                    Were only One.

You'll rhyme, and woo, and fight, and joke,
                    Perhaps you'll pun !
Such feats are ·never· done by folk
                    Before they're One.

Some day, too, you may have your joy,
              And envy none ;
Yes, you, yourself, may own a boy,
              Who isn't One.

He'll dance, and laugh, and crow, he'll do
              As you have done :
(You crown a happy home, tho' you
              Are only One).

But when he's grown shall you be here
              To share his fun,
And talk of times, when he (the dear !)
              Was.hardly One ?

. Dear Child, 'tis your poor lot to be
              My little son ;
I'm glad, tho' I am old, you see,—
              While you are

1876.

———◦◦◦———

LITTLE DINKY.

(A RHYME OF LESS THAN ONE.)

The hair she means to have is gold,
Her eyes are blue, she's twelve weeks old,
    Plump are her fists and pinky.
She fluttered down in lucky hour
From some blue deep in yon sky bower—
    I call her LITTLE DINKY.

A Tiny now, ere long she'll please
To totter at my parent-knees,
    And crow, and try to chatter:
And soon she'll take to fair white frocks,
And frisk about in shoes and socks,—
    Her totter changed to patter.

And soon she'll play, ay, soon enough,
At cowslip ball and blindman's-buff;
    And, some day, we shall find her
Grow weary of her toys—indeed
She'll fling them all aside, to heed
    A footstep close behind her.

And years to come she'll still be rich
In what is left, the joys with which
    Our love can aye supply us;
For hand in hand we'll sit us down
Right cheerfully, and let the town—
    This foolish town, go by us.

Dinky, we must resign our toys
To younger girls, to finer boys,—
    But we'll not care a feather:
For then (reflection's not regret)
Tho' you'll be rather old, we'll yet
    Be boy and girl together.

As I was climbing Ludgate Hill
I met a goose who dropt a quill,—
　　You see my thumb is inky ;—
I fell to scribble there and then,
And this is how I came to pen,
　　These rhymes on LITTLE DINKY.
1878.

* * *

STORY TELLERS.

Some two or three years ago I was dining out and
met S——, and I chanced to tell the company my
funny story of Aunt Amabel, that very gentle and be-
nign old being. I will relate it again ! My aunt was
on a visit to London, and had climbed into an omnibus
to go and hear the Reverend Baptist Noel preach, and
after a long delay she was obliged to remonstrate with
the conductor. He had beguiled her into his vehicle,
and then, having secured her, halted before a public-
house while the driver thoroughly enjoyed himself
within. The crushed worm *will* turn (though, by the
way, not if the crushing is done effectually), so my
aunt mildly expostulated with him for being 'really so
exceedingly dilatory.'

The point of the anecdote turns on the conductor
becoming exceedingly impertinent, and saying, ' Now,
this is too bad of you, old gal, a-comin' here, a-kickin'
up a row of a Sunday—you ought to be ashamed o'
yourself.' It so happened that my story fell rather flat,

nobody seemed to care much for it. Well, oddly enough, the very next day I met S—— at another dinner-party at another house. I suppose he had recognised the capabilities of my little anecdote, for we had not been five minutes in the room before he favoured the company with the whole of it (of course, he did not remember that I had narrated it—or else he was a more impudent fellow than I would even give him credit for). As S—— was very comical, and had the *art de narrer* in perfection, he sent the company into convulsions of laughter—which reminded me that when a man laughs he is not very merry but very proud. The only variations that he condescended to make in my story were the substitution of 'Spurgeon' for the Reverend Baptist Noel, and 'my old house-keeper' for Aunt Amabel—the last not altogether respectful to my virtuous relative.

A certain Mr. Archer, well known as an expert in drawing the long-bow, also at a dinner-party, was describing a man being washed overboard during a fearful hurricane in the Atlantic, and how, just as the poor wretch was sinking, Archer, with infinite presence of mind, threw him a hen-coop—'and,' said he, 'if I were to live ten thousand years I should never forget the agonised expression of that poor fellow's face as I threw him the hen-coop.' Then a person sitting opposite to Archer, gravely said, 'Are you quite sure Mr. 'Archer, you could never forget that man's face?'

D

'I am quite sure of it,' said Archer. 'Then,' said the man, slowly and solemnly, gazing at him, and then round upon the company, with his hand upon his breast, 'Look at me, sir, *I* am that man to whom you flung *that* hen-coop.' And of course everybody fell a-laughing.

Sir Arthur C. was telling long rhodomontade stories about America, and the Red Indians, at Lord Barrymore's table, and Barrymore (winking at the company) asked him—'Did you ever see anything of the *Chick-Chows?*'—'Oh, a good deal,' said Sir Arthur, 'a very cruel tribe, the *Chick-Chows.*' 'And the *Cherry-Chows,* eh?'—'Oh, very much among the *Cherry-Chows,*' continued Sir Arthur, 'the Cherry-Chows were singularly kind to my fellows.' 'And pray, Sir Arthur, did you see much of the *Tol-de-roddy-bow-wows?*' This was rather too much for Sir Arthur, who then, for the first time, perceived that Barrymore had been quizzing him.

This reminds me of another traveller who was describing the Indians, and their modes of life to a lady of an inquiring mind, and who said, 'Now about wig-wams, you know, are they so *very* venomous?'

Apropos of story-tellers, Charles Lamb describes a young man he was shut up with on board the old Margate Hoy—the greatest liar he had ever met. 'He was dark and handsome, with an officer-like assurance, and unsuppressible volubility of assertion.

He was none of your hesitating, half story-tellers, who
go on sounding your belief, and only giving you as
much as they see you can swallow at a time. He did
not stand shivering upon the brink, but was a hearty
thorough-paced liar, and plunged at once into the
depths of your credulity. I believe he made pretty
sure of his company, for we were a set of as unseasoned
Londoners as that time of day could have supplied.
Something, too, must be conceded to the *genius loci*.
Had the fellow told us half the legends on land, which
he favoured us with on the other element, I flatter myself the good sense of most of us would have revolted.
But we were in a new world, with everything unfamiliar
about us, and the time and the place disposed us to the
reception of any prodigious marvel whatsoever.

'He had been aide-de-camp (among other rare
accidents and fortunes) to a Persian Prince, and at one
blow had stricken off the head of the King of Carimania.
He, of course, married the Prince's daughter. I forget what unlucky turn in the politics of the Court, com-
bining with the loss of his consort, was the reason of
his quitting Persia ; but, with the rapidity of a magician,
he transported himself, along with his hearers, back to
England, where he was still found in the special confidence of illustrious ladies. There was some story of
a Princess, but, as I am not certain of her name, I
must leave it to the Royal Daughters of England to
settle the honour among themselves—in private. I

cannot call to mind half his pleasant wonders ; but I perfectly remember that in the course of his travels he had seen a phœnix, and he obligingly undeceived us of the vulgar error that there is but one of that species at a time, assuring us that they are by no means uncom-, mon in some parts of Upper Egypt,' &c., &c.

One story more, and I have done, and we will dismiss these cheery liars, for whom, I confess, I have a considerable weakness. My friend S—— was one of the kindest beings I ever knew. Alas ! he has gone over to the majority.

Now for 'Mr. Joseph Addison.' 'Two gentlemen— I believe, Mr. George Augustus Sala, and the late Mr. James Hannay—happened to be in a coffee-house where, for privacy, the seats were divided into separate boxes. They were extolling the character and writings of Addison, with all the enthusiasm which the subject deserved.. In the middle of their discourse a hungry, shabby-looking fellow suddenly popped his head round the corner from the next box, and said, with a very broad Irish accent, ' Your pardon, gentlemen, but my name's Joseph Addison, I am lineally descended from that great gentleman himself, and just now I have certain temporary embarrassments of a pecuniary nature, &c., &c., &c. Then Mr. Hannay or Mr. Sala, I do not know which, and anyhow I beg Mr. Sala's pardon, with perfect presence of mind and remarkable readiness of resource, at once replied to him thus :

'You have intruded yourself on our privacy, but, having heard what you have just said, I will merely remark that when Addison died he left an only daughter, and she was an idiot, and therefore, so far, there would seem to be some colour for the truth of your assertion, but seeing that this idiot daughter died in childhood, I am bound to say you are a thorough-paced impostor and liar.'

A DILEMMA.

St. Paul writes to Titus (ch. i. ver. 12) : 'One of themselves, even a prophet of their own, said, The Cretans are alway liars.'

If the prophet (Epimenides) was a liar (which, being a Cretan, he ought to have been), then this sentiment was false of the Cretans. If he was a truthful man, it was still untrue, because it proved that there *was* one Cretan (namely himself) who was not a liar.

CAPITAL IN THE WRONG PLACE.

A very High Church clergyman, in Norfolk, undertook to do duty for a neighbour, who, as it turned out, did not carry on the ceremonial of his Church in altogether a sympathetic manner. He was about to ascend the pulpit stairs when the Clerk plucked him by the sleeve, and whispered his hopes that he would not mind delivering his sermon from the reading desk, for, 'Your pardon, sir, but there's a hen tukkey a-settin' in the pŭl-pit!'

HIGH OR LOW CHURCH.

A clergyman, of Brownwich, called at the Inn to order dinner for a clerical meeting. ''igh Church or Low Church, sir?' said the waiter. 'What can that matter?' said the clergyman. 'Oh, werry important, sir,' says the waiter; ''igh Church—better wine, sir; Low Church—more wittles.'

THOMAS FULLER.

(1608—1661.)

FOOLS.

There are fools with little heads, and there are fools with big heads : in the one case there is no room for so much wit, and in the other case there is no wit for so much room.

THE GOOD YEOMAN.

The good yeoman is a gentleman in ore, whom the next age may see refined.

THE WOUNDED SOLDIER.

Halting is the stateliest march of a soldier.

WILLIAM COWPER.

I have lately seen some of Cowper's little poems, especially those to Mary Unwin, described as the love-songs of old age. Mr. F. T. Palgrave says of one of these : ' I know no sonnet more remarkable than this which records Cowper's gratitude to the lady whose affectionate care for many years gave what sweetness he could enjoy to a life radically wretched. Petrarch's sonnets have a more ethereal grace, and a more perfect finish ; Shakespeare's more passion ; Milton's stand supreme in stateliness ; Wordsworth's in depth and delicacy. But Cowper's unites with an exquisiteness in the turn of thought which the ancients would have called Irony, an intensity of pathetic tenderness peculiar to his loving and ingenuous nature. There is much mannerism, much that is unimportant or of now exhausted interest in his poems, but where he is great it is with that elementary greatness which rests on the most universal human feelings. Cowper is our highest master in simple pathos.

Cowper Poplar Field' is a very skilful effort of versification Byron, Moore, Campbell, and others, have written in this metre; but I think Cowper is the

most successful of all. It is the easiest metre in which
to write badly, but one of the most difficult in which
to write exceedingly well.

———◦———

TO HIS COY MISTRESS.

'Had we but world enough, and time—
This coyness, Lady, were no crime :
We would sit down, and think which way
To walk, and pass our long love's day.
Thou by the Indian Ganges' side
Should'st rubies find : I by the tide
Of Humber would complain. I would
Love you ten years before the flood ;
And you should, if you please, refuse
Till the conversion of the Jews.
My vegetable love should grow
Vaster than empires, and more slow.
An hundred years should go to praise
Thine eyes, and on thy forehead gaze :
Two hundred to adore each breast :
But thirty thousand to the rest.
An age at least to every part,
And the last age should show your heart.
For, Lady, you deserve this state ;
Nor would I love at lower rate.
    ' But at my back I always hear
Time's winged chariot hurrying near

And yonder all before us lye:
Deserts of vast eternity.
Thy beauty shall no more be found;
Nor, in thy marble vault, shall sound
My echoing song: then worms shall try
That long preserved virginity:
And your quaint honour turn to dust;
And into ashes all my lust.
The grave's a fine and private place,
But none, I think, do there embrace.
   ' Now, therefore, while the youthful hue
Sits on my skin like morning dew,
And while thy willing soul transpires
At every pore with instant fires,
Now let us sport us while we may:
And now, like amorous birds of prey,
Rather at once our time devour,
Than languish in his slow-chaped power.
Let us roll all our strength, and all
Our sweetness, up into one ball;
And tear our pleasures with rough strife,
Thorough the iron gates of life.
Thus, tho' we cannot make our sun
Stand still, yet we will make him run.'

Andrew Marvell (1620-1678.

I hope that all my readers will like this little
poem.

BULLS.

Bulls admit apparent relations that are not real.
The following is an unconscious self-contradiction :

1st Democrat.—Are not all men equal ? is not one
man just as good as another ?

2nd Democrat.—Aye, and better too !

———◇———

IRISH BULLS.

An Irish physician asserted that sterility was
hereditary in some Irish families.

A patriotic Irishman insisted that absenteeism was
the curse of Tipperary. 'The whole county,' said he,
'is swarming with 'em.'

———◇———

A SCOTTISH BULL.

'A Scottish Judge had occasion to consult a dentist,
and was courteously placed in the professional chair ;
but when the operator said, "You must now let me
put my fingers into your Lordship's mouth," his Lordship exclaimed, "Na, na ! ye'll aiblins *bite me*."'

' Scottish Life and Character.'

———◇———

WIT AND HUMOUR.

The Scots, as a people, possess a very peculiar, and a very delightful humour. It is seen at its best in the writings of Burns and Scott, and it may be met with in perfection in Dean Ramsay's 'Reminiscences,' but they would appear almost entirely to lack what is now usually understood by *wit*. At this moment, unless an exception is made in favour of Tobias Smollett, I cannot remember any strikingly witty Scottish writer—witty in the sense that Fuller and Donne, Butler and Swift, Congreve and Farquhar, Sheridan and O Keefe, and a host of other English and Irish writers were witty. It is probable that Charles Lamb and Sydney Smith recognised this limitation when they were so facetious about matter-of-fact Scots : and, if so, it would have been well if they had defined the kind of wit or humour of which they were treating.

Johnson, Lamb, and Sydney Smith were undeniable judges as to the quality of the article, and they made very merry at the expense of the Scots ; and this leads me to consider whether there may not be something in their national foibles which peculiarly lays them open to ridicule. One can hardly conceive an Edinburgh Mr. Pickwick.

GENIUS.

'The genius of the Spanish people is exquisitely subtle, without being at all acute, hence there is so much humour and so little wit in their literature. The genius of the Italians, on the contrary, is acute, profound and sensuous, but not subtle, hence what they think to be humorous is merely witty.

Men of genius are rarely much annoyed by the company of vulgar people, because they have a power of looking *at* such persons as objects of amusement of another race altogether. Few men of genius are keen, but almost every man of genius is subtle. To split a hair is no proof of subtlety, for subtlety acts in distinguishing differences, in showing that two things apparently one are in fact two, whereas to split a hair is to cause division, and not to ascertain difference.

'To carry on the feelings of childhood into the powers of manhood, to combine the child's sense of wonder and novelty with the appearances which every day, for perhaps forty years, has rendered familiar; this is the character and privilege of genius, and one of the marks which distinguishes genius from talent.'

S. T. Coleridge,

THE LAST LEAF.

' I saw him once before,
As he passed by the door,
            And again
The pavement stones resound,
As he totters o'er the ground
            With his cane.

'They say that in his prime,
Ere the pruning-knife of Time
                    Cut him down,
Not a better man was found
By the Crier on his round
                    Thro' the town.

'But now he walks the streets,
And he looks at all he meets
                    Sad and wan,
And he shakes his feeble head,
That it seems as if he said,
                    "They are gone."

'*The mossy marbles rest*
On the lips that he has prest
                    In their bloom,
And the names he loved to hear
Have been carved for many a year
                    On the tomb.

'My grandmamma has said,—
Poor old lady, she is dead
                    Long ago,—
That he had a Roman nose,
And his cheek was like a rose
                    In the snow.

' But now his nose is thin,
And it rests upon his chin
    Like a staff,.
And a crook is in his back,
And a melancholy crack
    In his laugh.

' I know it is a sin
For me to sit and grin
    At him here;
But the old three-cornered hat,
And the breeches, and all that,
    Are so queer !

' And if I should live to be
The last leaf upon the tree
    In the spring,—
Let them smile, as I do now,
At the old forsaken bough
    Where I cling.'

        O. W. Holmes.

Dr. Holmes is very popular is England as a prose writer, and as a poet he is also much admired, but not so much as he ought to be, and yet he seems to have most of the qualities to make an author popular. Perhaps the many-headed beast would like to have its nostrils tickled with more highly seasoned stuff than Dr. Holmes cares to give them.

The lines quoted above are all very happy, but especially the fourth stanza, and the conclusion of the sixth. I have long had a kindly affection for this poem, and feel much indebted to Dr. Holmes, and here tender him my thanks.

MY GUARDIAN ANGEL.

'Abra was ready when I called her name,
And tho' 1 called another Abra came.'

Some eight years ago I called on certain friends in Pentonville (I do not care to reveal the exact address) ; they were not at home ; however, as I had come a long distance, and really wished to see them, I asked the servant to let me wait their return. This hand-maid was past her giddy youth, but had not nearly arrived at middle age. Some people might have called her comely, and some attractive ; *I* found her anything but cordial ; in fact, she had a slightly chilling manner, as if she was not immensely pleased to see me, and would not break her heart if she never saw me again. However, in I walked, and was taken to a drawing-room, on the ground-floor, with French windows (open) to the garden.

The apartment was gorgeously furnished. Gold wall-paper, sumptuous hangings, and an aggressive crimson and orange carpet. It was brand new, of the

kind which, I think, is called *velvet pile*. There were
books on the inlaid tables, depressing books—Books of
Beauty, Views in the Holy Land, and Gems from our
Poets, all elaborately bound. Humming-birds were
stifling under glass shades, frail carved ivory ab-
surdities, only waiting for some one to smash them,
and magnificent paper knives, smelling-bottles, and all
the rest of it, in velvet cases, but there was no inkstand
and no writing material.

I resented this. Eight years ago—alas, I was eight
years younger than I am now, and rhymes were then
more often trotting in my head—it happened that
such became the case as I sat waiting for my friends,
and I felt if I did not at once secure them they might
be lost to me, and for ever. I had no pencil, and only
the back of a letter. So, rather cautiously, for I felt
ashamed of what I was doing, I opened the drawing-
room door, and stole across the passage to the library.
There I found pens and a gigantic glass inkstand. It
was somewhat this shape :—

I had never seen the form before, and I am not
ambitious of beholding it again. I bore it across the
hall, and as far as the centre of the drawing-room,
and then, all of a sudden, without any warning, the
lower portion (till that moment I had thought the

bloated monster was one piece of glass) detached itself from that which I held in my hand, and to which it had hitherto clung corroded, and fell to the floor, rolling over and over, along the wretched crimson and orange velvet pile, and emptying its ample contents as it rolled.

Can you conceive my feelings? I spun round the room in an agony. I tore at the bell, then at the other bell, then at both the bells, then I dashed into the library and rang the bells there, and then back again to the drawing-room. The maid who had admitted me, came up almost immediately, looking as calm as possible, and when she saw the mischief, *she seemed, all at once, to rise to the gravity of the occasion.* She did not say a word—she did not even look dismayed—but, in answer to my frenzied appeal, she smiled and vanished. In the twinkling of a bed-post, however, she was back again with hot water, soap, sponge, &c., and was soon mopping up the copious stains with a damp flannel, kneeling, and looking beautiful as she knelt.

Then did I throw myself into a chair, exhausted with excitement, and, I may say agony of mind, and I said to myself, 'Good heavens, if the blessed creature does really help me in this frightful emergency, I will give her a sovereign. . It will be cheap at a sovereign ; yes, she shall have her 20s.' Well, what with sponging and dabbing, the great black stains began gradually to

E

wax fainter, and my spirits revived in proportion, and, all the while, this angelic being spoke so cheerfully, and had altogether such a fetching air (I believe that is the correct expression) that I longed to twine my arms about her modest waist and assure her how deeply I respected her.

> Old as I am, for ladies' love unfit,
> The power of beauty I remember yet.

However, at this juncture, I am almost ashamed to confess it, I began to revolve in my mind whether ten shillings might not be a sufficient recompense, for, after all, she had not been much more than ten minutes about the whole affair. Well, the scrubbing went on, and then she took to her brush, and in certainly less than twenty minutes, the stains had *entirely disappeared*, and my Guardian Angel rose to her feet, and asked me, with a quiet little smile, as though it were all the most natural thing in the world, if I should like to have a cup of tea. I accepted her pious offer with joy and gratitude, and there I sat me down and gazed complacently at the again gorgeous crimson and orange velvet pile, and sipped my tea, and by the time I had finished it (and my rhyme) my friends made their appearance.

You may suppose that at first I felt a little uncomfortable, especially so, when in something less than five seconds my good friend bawled to his wife,

'Millicent, Millicent, look here! now this is too bad, just look at my carpet!' (my soul died within me!) I had my back to him. He was not far from the window; he seemed close to the spot where the catastrophe had happened. 'Yes,' said he, 'they *will* leave the windows open, and your brute of a pug has brought all this filthy gravel in on his paws.' I breathed again, and feeling constrained to say something, I observed, with a sickly smile, 'So our friend Oscar is very particular about his carpet, eh?' 'Particular,' said his little wife, 'indeed he is particular, and awfully so just now, for this is a new purchase, it was only laid down yesterday. You don't know how awfully fidgety Oscar is about his carpets—won't you have some tea?' This was not reassuring! I lost heart, I became completely demoralised, and I am ashamed to say I made a hurried excuse, and bolted out of the room, and out of the house, without telling my friends a word of what had occurred. On my honour I had intended to tell them, but could not muster up courage to begin; indeed, they never gave me the chance of doing so.

As I journeyed home I speculated whether that dreadful stain, like the crimson traces of a foul murder, might not reappear next day, or, horrid thought, whether my beloved Parlour Maid might not betray me. I feared she might do so; I felt she would be justified in doing so—indeed, that it was her bounden duty to do so; therefore, and before I went to bed,

I wrote my friends a penitential, I might almost describe it as, a pitiful letter, and gave a full and true account of what had happened. I threw myself on their mercy,—but ....

I forgot to say that I presented my Guardian Angel with a handsome donation of five shillings. And this is the end of a true story.

FAMILIARITY BREEDS CONTEMPT.

Robert McQueen (Lord Braxfield), a Scottish judge of the old school, playing at whist, exclaimed to a lady of rank, his partner, and of whose play he did not entirely approve, 'What are ye doin', ye —— auld ——?' and then suddenly recollecting himself, said, 'Your pardon's begged, my Lady, *I took ye for my ain wife.*'

Some of the merit of this little anecdote is its extreme raciness ; so I have been careful to omit the expletive and epithet, in order that the intelligent reader may select those which he, or she, may consider the most effective. The story is given in Mr. Trevelyan's most admirable biography of his uncle, Lord Macaulay.

AN UNFEELING RASCAL.

Old Hopkinson was walking in London streets when a man suddenly approached, snatched off his hat, and bolted with it. Hopkinson gave chase, and another man, who had observed the outrage, joined him. Away they both ran. At last old Hopkinson stopped, being completely out of breath, but the man who had joined him, encouraged him to go on. 'Run a little longer, sir,' said he. 'No,' gasped old Hopkinson, 'I can't.' 'Can't you run a step farther, sir?' said the man. 'No,' gasped old Hopkinson, 'not a step.' 'Then,' said the unfeeling rascal, 'hang you, I'll have your wig'—and he twitched off poor old Hopkinson's wig, and disappeared.

SURNAMES.

I very often see the name of *Pursey* over a tailor's shop, No. 4, Swallow Street, Regent Street, and I have no reason for doubting that the owner, though only the ninth part of a man, is an excellent tradesman, not to say an artist, and, to judge by the way he spells his name, we may presume that he does not go in for giving himself the airs which would be perfectly excusable in the cadet of a powerful and ancient family. Certainly, the name, as I read it over his place of

business, has nothing special to recommend it ; and
this leads me to reflect how much the beauty or ugli-
ness or dignity of a name springs from its associations.
There is nothing noble in the name of *Pursey.* Anson
and Nelson are well-sounding titles, yet, after all, one is
only the son of 'Ann' and the other of 'Nel.' What
should we think of 'Pitt' and 'Fox' without their
illustrious surroundings ? In reality they are very poor
names. Surely there ought to be a considerable
future for the queer name of Cobden.

You hear the Earl of Mar announced, and in
imagination you are at once transported to the dim
romance of our early Scottish History. What a proud
title ! [1] but *mar*, in itself, is no better than *jar*, and
not half so fine as the Right Honourable the Earl of
Marmalade, K.G.

'The Blues' happen to be mentioned, the sound
is rather overpowering ; all the glory of H.M. Life
Guards, their gold helmets and social splendours, are
at once almost dazzling, but is there any such feeling
as regards *the Browns.* I think Judas ought to be a
pretty name, and what say you to Jezebel? In England the plebeians have the shorter names. Planta-
genet is more patrician than Dick (the briefest-sounding
name I know). I am assured it is entirely the reverse
of this in China, where the most exalted personage in

[1] 'An eye like Ma's to threaten and command ! '

the realm has next to no name at all—only a *click*—
very like 'Dick,' (but shorter) more like that noise
.which people make to urge along their cattle.

CHARLES FOX.

'In his tour to Switzerland, Mr. Fox gave me two
days of free and private society. He seemed to feel
and even to envy the happiness of my situation, while
I admired the powers of a superior man, as they are
blended in his attractive character with the softness
and simplicity of a child. Perhaps no human being
was ever more perfectly exempted from the taint of
malevolence, vanity and falsehood.'—

Edmund Gibbon (1737—1794).

A MA FUTURE.

'Where waitest thou,
Lady, I am to love? Thou comest not,
Thou knowest of my sad and lowly lot—
I looked for thee ere now!

'It is the May,
And each sweet sister soul hath found its brother,
Only we two seek fondly each the other,
And seeking still delay.

'Where art thou, sweet?'
I long for thee as thirsty lips for streams,
O gentle promised angel of my dreams,
 Why do we never meet?

'Thou art as I,
Thy soul doth wait for mine as mine for thee;
We cannot live apart, must meeting be
 Never before we die?

'Dear soul, not so,
For time doth keep for us some happy years,
And God hath portion'd us our smiles and tears,
 Thou knowest, and I know.

'Therefore I bear
This winter-tide as bravely as I may,
Patiently waiting for the bright spring day
 That cometh with thee, dear.

''Tis the May light
That crimsons all the quiet college gloom,
May it shine softly in thy sleeping room,
 And so, dear wife, good night.'

Edwin Arnold.

RELIGIOUS TRAINING.

A Presbyterian minister concluded his pulpit exhortations, and arguments on free will, predestination, ' foreknowledge absolute,' etc., with the following highly consoling words '*ye canna be gude, an', if ye were gude, it wad do ye na gude.*' This story might divert some people, but it is no laughing matter for my friend Eugenius.

Eugenius has a very sensitive, and perhaps a spiritual nature, and I presume he has a sceptical mind. He tells me that his very early Calvinistic, and gloomy religious training and teaching, and perpetual chapel-going, has warped and embittered his soul, in such a manner, and to such a degree, that, I fear, I shall never see Eugenius in a haven of spiritual peace. It is remarkable how that early teaching sticks by a man, and, as it were, takes possession of him, and how, as he grows old, he reverts to the hopes or the fears of his childhood. What a blessing, then, if the influence has been a healthy one !

The other day I heard that whimsical fellow, G——, make a rather foolish remark, to the effect that the pleasure of *not* going to church was a pleasure that *never* palled. I should have liked to have sent his address to my poor Eugenius.

EPITAPH.

ON AN ANCESTOR OF DAVID ELGINBROD.

Here lie I, Martin Elginbrod.
Hae mercy on my soul, Lord God,
As I wad do were I Lord God,
And ye were Martin Elginbrod.

L'ENFER.

'Ne nous imaginons pas que l'enfer consiste dans
ces étangs de feu et de soufre, dans ces flammes éter-
nellement dévorantes, dans cette rage, dans ce déses-
poir, dans cet horrible grincement de dents. L'enfer,
si nous l'entendons, c'est le péché même : l'enfer, c'est
d'être éloigné de Dieu.'   Bishop Bossuet (1627—1704).

GASTIBELZA.

' Gastibelza, l'homme à la carabine,
              Chantait ainsi :
Quelqu'un a-t-il connu Doña Sabine ?
              Quelqu'un d'ici ?
Dansez, chantez, villageois ! la nuit gagne
              Le Mont Falu.
Le vent qui vient à travers la montagne
              Me rendra fou.

'Quelqu'un de vous a-t-il connu Sabine,
  Ma Señora?
Sa mère était la vieille maugrabine
  d'Antequera
Qui chaque nuit criait dans la Tour Magne
  Comme un hibou . . . —
Le vent qui vient à travers la montagne
  Me rendra fou.

'Dansez, chantez! Des biens que l'heure envoie
  Il faut user.
Elle était jeune, et son œil plein de joie
  Faisait penser.—
(A ce vieillard qu'un enfant accompagne
  Jetez un sou ! . . . —)
Le vent qui vient à travers la montagne
  Me rendra fou.

'Vraiment, la reine eût, près d'elle, été laide
  Quand, vers le soir,
Elle passait sur le pont de Tolède
  En corset noir.
Un chapelet du temps de Charlemagne
  Ornait son cou . . . —
Le vent qui vient à travers la montagne
  Me rendra fou.

'Le roi disait, en la voyant si belle,
          A son neveu :
" Pour un baiser, pour un sourire d'elle,
          Pour un cheveu,
Infant Don Ruy, je donnerais l'Espagne
          Et le Pérou ! "
Le vent qui vient à travers la montagne
          Me rendra fou.

'Je ne sais pas si j'aimais cette dame,
          Mais je sais bien
Que, pour avoir un regard de son âme,
          Moi, pauvre chien,
J'aurais gaîment passé dix ans au bagne
          Sous le verrou . . .
Le vent qui vient à travers la montagne
          Me rendra fou.

'Un jour d'été quand tout était lumière,
          Vie et douceur,
Elle s'en vint jouer dans la rivière
          Avec sa sœur :
Je vis le pied de sa jeune compagne
          Et son genou . . . —
Le vent qui vient à travers la montagne
          Me rendra fou.

'Quand je voyais cet enfant, moi, le pât
        De ce canton,
Je croyais voir la belle Cléopâtre
        Qui, nous dit-on,
Menait César, empereur d'Allemagne,
        Par le licou . . . —
Le vent qui vient à travers la montagne
        Me rendra fou.

'Dansez, chantez, villageois, la nuit tombe !
        Sabine un jour
A tout vendu, sa beauté de colombe
        Et son amour,
Pour l'anneau d'or du comte de Saldagne,
        Pour un bijou . . . —
Le vent qui vient à travers la montagne
        Me rendra fou.

'Sur ce vieux banc souffrez que je m'appuie,
        Car je suis las.
Avec ce comte elle s'est donc enfuie !
        Enfuie, hélas !
Par le chemin qui va vers la Cerdagne,
        Je ne sais où . . . —
Le vent qui vient à travers la montagne
        Me rendra fou.

'Je la voyais passer de ma demeure,
        Et c'était tout.
Mais à présent je m'ennuie à toute heure,
        Plein de dégoût,
Rêveur, oisif, l'âme dans la campagne,
        La dague au clou . . . —
Le vent qui vient à travers la montagne
        M'a rendu fou !'   Victor Hugo.

TAKING STOCK.

A worthy man, with a little capital, set up a wool-mill. Coming home one evening, at the end of the first year, he appeared in great good humour, and meeting his wife at the door, he said, 'Ye'll mak' a drop tea till's, gudewife.' Tea was then a considerable rarity and looked upon in the light of a luxury. 'Ou, ay,' says the wife, 'but what's ado wi' ye the nicht?' ' Eh, 'oman, the miliy's doin' fine. She's cleared hersel' a'ready, and somethin' forby.' The next night he was looking rather disconsolate, and on his wife inquiring if again he was to have tea—'Na, na,' says he, 'nae mair o' thot stuff, that stupid blockhead Jock, in balancin' the books, added in the *Anno Domini* along wi' the punds.'

· This reminds me of the small trader who revealed that he had sold for only two sous what he had bought

for two and a half sous—and he was told that at that
rate, he would ruin himself. 'Non,' said he. 'Je me
sauve sur la quantité.'

———◦○◦———

THE BULLY.

At old Bliss's school there was a big, foulmouthed
Bully, who tyrannised over the other boys ; and he held
the lesser fellows in such abject subjection, that, long
before the arrival of their plum-cakes, they had been
heavily mortgaged to propitiate him. He was a
regular land-pirate of the most shameless type, he
preyed upon our toffy and tarts, he confiscated our
neckerchiefs and knives, and he even made free with
our pocket-money. I can see him now, he was fat,
with a broad nose and face. I remember how he
would tear down the centre of the long dormitory,'
when the younger ones were a-bed, and give a yell,
and a great laugh as he dragged the bedclothes off
each boy as he passed.

I can conceive no wickedness of which this young
monster could not have been capable : and anybody
might have supposed him to be utterly callous, and in-
capacitated for any kind of remorse. On looking back
I cannot help suspecting he was a coward (even now
I hardly dare to say what I think of him, lest he should
still be alive, and *this should meet his eyes*). Yes, he

was a coward, he would tempt other boys to mischief
for which he had not the pluck himself. It was he
who incited Wentworth to convey the bumble-bees to
church in a whity-brown paper bag, and then let
them out, one by one, during the sermon.

There was a hideous old usher (I call him old, but,
really, I do not the least know whether he was thirty
or sixty) whom we branded as '*Gums*' (he had a
horrid way of grinning when he called us up to be
flogged). This usher was a mysterious animal. I
fancy now that he may have been deadly poor, for
there were thick worsted bell-ropes in his bed-chamber,
and it was darkly whispered that when he hadn't any
tobacco, he would cut off pieces of the bell-ropes, and
put them into his pipe, and smoke them. Yes, his
position was shrouded in mystery; he remained, high
and dry, up at the school-house during the holidays,
and the only circumstance I know to the credit of the
Bully was that he bought some mustard and cress
(with another boy's money) and sowed GUMS in
gigantic characters under Gums's window, the day
before the school broke up. I doubt if he would have
ventured to do this if it had not been his last half at
the school. Yes, I believe the Bully was an arrant
coward, and now I will tell you why I have wasted so
much of your time upon him; and remember, dear
reader, I am about to deal with a serious subject—a

very serious subject, and, believe me, I do so with all reverence ; pray remember this.

There was a certain small apartment at the corner of the schoolroom, which was called 'Old Gums's crib,' where the biggest boys washed their hands and brushed their hair during the day. It was a darkish room, and, one afternoon, when I chanced to be alone there, the Bully came up to me abruptly, and said, with abject terror in his face,—' I say, you fellow, look here, I hope I haven't sinned against the Holy Ghost.' This was all he said, he then grasped me by the arm, as he repeated the startling question and glared at me, and then, as I was taken aback, and also in considerable alarm, and did not reply, he gave me a vicious kick, which sent me flying.

I found out afterwards that there was hardly a little boy in the school to whom the poor wretch, in his agony, had not, at some time or other, put the same question (and given the same kick) and tried, as it were, to get comfort out of him. His name was. . . .

WHAT WIGHT HE LOVED.

'Shall I tell you whom I love ?
  Hearken then awhile to me ;
And if such a woman move
  As I now shall versifie ;

F

Be assured, 'tis she, or none
That I love, and love alone.

' Nature did her so much right,
    As she scorns the help of art,
In as many virtues dight
    As ere yet imbraced a hart.
So much good so truly tride,
Some for lesse were deified.

' Wit she hath without desire
    To make knowne how much she hath ;
And her anger flames no higher
    Than may fitly sweeten wrath.
Full of pity as may be,—
Tho' perhaps not so to me !

' Reason masters every sense,
    And her virtues grace her birth ;
Lovely as all excellence,
    Modest in her most of mirth :
Likelihood enough to prove
Onely worth could kindle love.

' Such she is ;—and if you know
    Such a one as I have sung,
Be she browne, or faire, or so,
    That she be but somewhile young ;
Be assured, 'tis she, or none
That I love, and love alone.'

William Browne (1590-1645).

WHAT IS A MIRACLE?

Clergyman. What is a miracle?

Boy. Dunno.

Clergyman. Well, if the sun were to shine in the middle of the night, what should you say it was?

Boy. The moon.

Clergyman. But if you were told it was the sun, what should you say it was?

Boy. A lie.

Clergyman. I don't tell lies. Suppose I told you it was the sun, what would you say then?

Boy. That yer wasn't *sober*.

A LENGTHY PAUSE.

An old gentleman, riding over Putney Bridge, turned round to his servant, and said, 'Do you like eggs, John?' 'Yes, Sir,' answered John. Here their conversation ended. The same old gentleman, riding across the same bridge, the next year, again turned to John, and said, 'How?' 'Poached, Sir,' was John's instant reply. This is the longest pause on record.

It is evident here the makings of an excellent domestic. A really good servant should never be out of the way.

STATISTICS OF FRIENDSHIP.

Apropos of the loss, of friends, some one, in the presence of Morgan, the great calculator of lives, deplored that he had been bereaved of so many friends, mentioning their number, in a certain space of time. Morgan, for the moment, said nothing, but taking down a huge book from his office shelf, and consulting it, coolly remarked, 'So you ought, Sir, and three more.'

A SUITABLE BRIDE.

My friend Admiral E. E., shortly after his return from a cruise, met an old acquaintance in the streets of ——, who said, after the usual salutations had passed, 'They tell me, Admiral, that ye had got married.' The Admiral, hoping for a compliment, replied, 'Why, Baillie, I'm getting on, I'm not so young as I was, you and none of the girls will have me.' On which Baillie, with perfect good faith and simplicity, replied, Admiral, I was na evenin' yer to a lassie, there's mony a fine, respeckit, *half worn widow* be glad to tak ye.'

SONG.

'Love in fantastic triumph sat
   Whilst bleeding hearts around him flow'd,
From whom fresh pains he did create,
   And strange tyrannic power he showed.
From thy bright eyes he took his fires,
   Which round about in sport he hurl'd ;
But 'twas from mine he took desires,
   Enough t' undo the amorous world.

' From me he took his sighs and tears,
   From thee his pride and cruelty ;
From me his languishment and fears,
   And every killing dart from thee :
Thus, thou and I, the god have arm'd,
   And set him up a deity ;
But my poor heart alone is harm'd
   Whilst thine the victor is, and free.'

From *Abdelazer, or the Moor's Revenge*, Aphra Behn (1642 1689).

TOM CAMPBELL.

A great many years ago an acquaintance of mine,
a festive but very stupid fellow, who, to use one of his
own homely similes, had no more feeling for poetry
than a cow would have for a clean shirt, told me that
he had known Tom Campbell He used to meet him

at a small club in (I think) Regent Street : where he, and others, occasionally dined. Poor Tom would sometimes take a little too much wine. In those days almost everybody did so, and my acquaintance said that on one occasion, after dinner, Campbell got up and staggered towards the door. There were some providential pillars that supported the roof of the apartment, and he reached them with difficulty, and, having done so, he clung to one of them tenaciously, fearing to go further and afraid to return—and that he remained there ! 'And,' said I, who worshipped Campbell with all a boy's enthusiasm, 'what did you do ?' ' Oh,' says he, ' we left him there, but every now and again, you know, we would *flick* a walnut at him.'

Campbell is well known to have been an interesting converser ; he rarely left you without having made some observation that was singularly suggestive, and which lingered agreeably in the memory. It was he who said

> To live in hearts we leave behind
> Is not to die !

but the graceless animal (my acquaintance) knew nothing of this, he was only able to tell me that Campbell was a little fellow, that he spoke with a broad Scottish accent, and that he wore a wig.

> Yet wandering I found in my ruinous walk,
> By the dial-stone aged and green,
> One rose of the wilderness left on its stalk
> To mark where a garden had been.

A SYMPATHETIC DAIRYMAID.

Sir James ―― on one occasion had ventured to buy a cow, without consulting his dairy-maid, a great authority on such matters : when the new purchase was first exhibited to her she found herself divided between her love of truth, and her amiable desire not to wound the feelings of her beloved master by expressing her candid opinion. She looked meditatively at the new acquisition, and then said, 'She's a bonnie beastie' (pause). 'She's some hee (high) at the root o' the tail' (longer pause)—'*but* we're a' that !'

DANGERS OF THE (FAR) WESTERN CIRCUIT.

'We remember reading in an American newspaper, some years ago, that the United States lost one of their most upright and erudite judges by bees, which stung him to death in a wood while he was going the circuit. About a year afterwards, we read in the same newspaper, "We are afraid we have just lost another judge by bees," and then followed a somewhat frightful description of the assassination of the American Blackstone by these insects.'

Professor Wilson (1785-1854).

ATALANTA IN CAMDEN TOWN.

' Ay, 'twas here, on this spot,
    In that summer of yore,
Atalanta did not
    Vote my presence a bore,
Nor reply, to my tenderest talk, she had "heard a
    that nonsense before."

' She'd the brooch I had bought,
    And the necklace and sash on,
And her heart, as I thought,
    Was alive to my passion :
And she'd done up her hair in the style that the
    Empress had brought into fashion.

' I had been to the play
    With my pearl of a Peri :
But, for all I could say,
    She declared she was weary,
That " the place was so crowded and hot," and she
    "couldn't abide that Dundreary."

' Then I thought " 'tis for me
    That she whines and she whimpers,
And it soothed me to see
    Those sensational simpers :
And I said, "This is *scrumptious*,"—a phrase I had
    learned from the Devonshire shrimpers.

And I vowed, "'Twill be said
    I'm a fortunate fellow,
When the breakfast is spread,
    When the topers are mellow,
When the foam of the bride-cake is white, and the
    fierce orange blossoms are yellow."

'Oh, that languishing yawn !
    Oh, those eloquent eyes !
I was drunk with the dawn
    Of a splendid surmise—
I was stung by a look—I was slain by a tear, by a
    tempest of sighs.

'And I whispered, "I guess
    The sweet secret thou keepest,
And the dainty distress
    That thou wistfully weepest :
And the question is 'license or banns?'—Though
    undoubtedly banns are the cheapest."

' Then her white hand I clasp'd,
    And with kisses I crowned it.
But she glared, and she gasp'd,
    And she mutter'd, " Confound it ! "
Or at least it was something like that, but the noise
    of the omnibus drown'd it.   Lewis Carroll.

SUPERSTITION.

James Mitchell was my gamekeeper, and he complained to me that his cow was 'witched.' I told him
he was talking nonsense, that the cow had merely
gone off its milk in consequence of his wife being
confined to bed, and the cow given over to the
management of his daughter, a girl of fourteen years
of age. He said, ' I ken weel wha has " witched " my
coo, it wasna for naething that Mistress Watson stood
glowrin' at her wi' her arms at her sides.'

I advised him to be careful as to what he said, as
Mrs. Watson's son, being a writer, would certainly
prosecute him for libel. ' Na, na,' said he, ' I ken weel
what I say. I ken it wor her, for one day I gied to the
kennel to feed my daugs, an' I laid my gun again' the
rails—and what should run past but a hare: there
was na a daug in the kennel that didna cower when
that hare run past.' (He was always accustomed to
flog them if they chased hares.) I up wi' my gun,
and takes a good aim at it, and I didna miss it, but
the shot was never cast that would kill *that* hare. The
next day was the Sarbbath, and I gangs up to the
kirk, an' wha' should I see but Mistress Watson wi
her heed tied up. . . . *I kennt I hadna missed her!*'

C. L. C. B.

A MAN OF FEW WANTS.

An Irishman with a very scanty wardrobe, was strongly advised to buy a portmanteau which was offered him at what appeared an exceedingly reasonable price. Said Pat, 'But what should I do wid it?' 'Why, put your clothes into it, to be sure,' said his adviser. 'What?' says Pat, quite puzzled—'What? and go naked!''

OLIVER GOLDSMITH.

Thomas Campbell said of Goldsmith's poetry : 'It enjoys a calm and steady popularity,' (I fear this is hardly the case just now,) 'and it presents us, within its narrow limits, a distinct and unbroken view of poetical delightfulness. His descriptions and sentiments have the pure zest of nature. He is refined without false delicacy, and correct without insipidity.'

I suppose everybody knows Goldsmith's delightful 'Elegy on a Mad Dog.' It has been remarked that *Manon Lescault* is the great-great-grandmamma of the modern school of French Novel, of which *La Dame aux Camélias* is typical; surely this elegy of Goldsmith's might bear the same relationship to many of Thomas Hood's inimitable comicalities. It is not so vigorous in versification, it may not be so wildly or fancifully comic, but it is more delicate, and, if I may

be allowed the expression, much more *gracious*, and if
it were read now, for the first time, it might pass for a
very happy specimen of the gifted author of ' Nelly
Gray.' I should like to think that Goldsmith and
Hood were now discussing it, pleasantly, in some
spiritual *cosmos!*

Perhaps there is no couplet in English rhyme
more perspicuously condensed than Goldsmith's on
the French nation :

' They please—are pleased—they give to get esteem,
   Till, seeming blest, they grow to what they seem.'

Goldsmith *excelled* as novelist, poet, dramatist,
essayist, and satirist, and, in this respect, I doubt if
he is equalled by any English writer.

THOMAS HOOD'S COMICALITY.

Thomas Hood plays off his tricks on the most
knowing readers : he carries on his double-dealing
with apparently the utmost simple-mindedness.

' And Christians love in the turf to lie,
   Not in watery graves to be—
Nay the very fishes would *sooner* die
   On the land than in the sea.'

He treats logic with a mock ceremonial of respect, as
in the case of

His head was turned, *and so* he chewed
His pig-tail till he died.

Hood supplied titles for sham books in the Chatsworth
library ; he invented many, here are four of them :

Novel.—Percy Vere, in forty volumes.
The Life of Zimmerman—by himself.
Tadpoles—or tales out of my own head.
Voltaire, Volney, Volta—three vols.

———•◇•———

A LETTER OF DEAN SWIFT.

'Dublin, Oct. 6, 1694.

' May it please your Honor,--

' That I might not continue by any means the many
troubles I have given you, I have all this while avoyded
one, which I fear proves necessary at last. I have taken
all due methods to be ordayned and one Time of Ordination is allready elapsed since my Arrivall without
effecting it. Two or three Bishops, acquaintances of
our Family, have signified to me and them that after so
long a standing in the University it is admired I have
not entered upon something or other (above half the
Clergy in this Town being my Juniors) and that it,
being so many Years since I left this Kingdom, they
could not admit me to the Ministry without some certificate of my Behavior where I lived : And my Lord

Archbishop of Dublin was pleased to say a good deal
of this kind to me Yesterday, concluding against all 'I
had to answer that He expected I should have a Certificate from Your Honor of my Conduct in your Family.
The sense I am in, how low I am fallen in Your Honor's
Thoughts has denyed me Assurance enough to beg
this Favor till I find it impossible to avoyd, And I
entreat Your Honor to understand, that no Person is
admitted to a Living here, without some Knowledge of
His Abilityes for it ; which it being reckon'd impossible
to judge in those who are not ordained, the usuall
Method is to admit them first to some small Reader's
Place till by Preaching upon Occasions they can value
themselves for better Preferment : This (without great
Friends) is so generall that if I were four score years
old, I must go the same way; and should at that age
be told, every one must have a Beginning. I entreat
that Your Honor will consider this, and will please to
send me some Certificate of my Behavior during almost
three years in Your Family : Wherein I shall stand in
need of all Your Goodness to excuse my many Weaknesses and Follyes and Oversights, much more to say
any Thing to my Advantage. The Particulars expected
of me, are what relate to Morals and Learning, and
the Reasons of quitting Your Honor's family, that is,
whether the last was occasioned by any ill Actions of
mine. They are all entirely left to Your Honor's

Mercy, tho' in the first, I think I cannot reproach myself any further than for Infirmityes.

'This is all I dare beg at present from Your Honor, under Circumstances of Life not worth your Regard : What is left me to wish (next to the Health and Felicity of Your Honor and Family) is. that Heaven would one Day allow me the Opportunity to leave my Acknowledgments at your feet, for so many Favors I have received, which, whatever effect they have had upon my Fortune, shall never fayl to have the greatest upon my Mind, in approving myself upon all occasions

'Your Honor's most obedient and most dutifull Servant   ' J. SWIFT.

' I beg my most humble duty and Service, be presented to my Ladyes, Your Honor's Lady and Sister.

'The ordination is appointed by the Arch-Bishop by the Beginning of November, so that if Your Honor will not grant this Favor immediatly I fear it will come too late.

'For the Honorable Sr William Temple, Bart., at His House at Moor Park near Farnham in Surrey, England.

' By way of London.'

₊*₊ This letter has never before been printed *in extenso*. I lent it to Mr. John Forster, but not soon enough to appear in his fragment of the Life of Swift.

I have a short note in Dean Swift's autograph
addressed to Alexander Pope, in which, after referring
to Lord Peterborough and Dr. Arbuthnot, he says : ' I
am weary of the Town, so that the kind lodging in
your Heart must be large indeed if it holds me; mine
cannot hold the Esteem and Friendship I have for
you.'

On the back of this note is written, in Pope's autograph, the following reflections : 'A King—a scarecrow
of straw, yet protects your corn.'

'A fine Lady is like a Catt, when young the most
gamesome and lively of all creatures—when old, the
most melancholy.'

A FAIRY FUNERAL.

' There it was on a little river island, that once,
whether sleeping or waking I know not, I saw celebrated a fairy's funeral. First, I heard small pipes
playing, as if no bigger than hollow rushes that
whisper in the night winds, and more piteous than
aught that trills from earthly instrument was the scarce
audible dirge. It seemed to pass over the stream,
every foam-bell emitting a plaintive note, till the fairy
anthem floated over our couch, and then alighting,
without footsteps, among the heather.

' The pattering of little feet was then heard, as if

living creatures were arranging themselves in order,
and then there was nothing but a more ordered hymn.
The harmony was like the melting of musical dew-
drops, and sung, without words, of sorrow and death.
I opened my eyes, or, rather, sight came to them when
closed, and dream was vision. Hundreds of creatures,
no taller than the crest of a lapwing, and all hanging
down their veiled heads, stood in a circle, in a green
plot among the rocks. In the midst of the circle, was
a bier, framed, as it seemed, of flowers, unknown to the
Highland Hills ; and on the bier a fairy, lying with un-
covered face pale as a lily, and motionless as the snow.
The dirge grew fainter, and fainter, and then died away.
Then two of the creatures came from the circle, and
took their station one at the head, and the other at the
foot of the bier. They sang alternate measures not
louder than the twittering of the awakened woodlark,
before it goes up the dewy air, but dolorous and full of
the desolation of death.

'The flower-bier stirred—for the spot on which it
lay sank slowly down, and in a few moments the green
sward was smooth as ever, the very dews glittering
above the buried fairy. A cloud passed over the moon,
and, with a choral lament, the funeral troop sailed
duskily away, heard afar off, so still was the midnight
solitude of the glen. Then the disenthralled Orchy
began to rejoice as before, through all her streams and

falls, and at the sudden leaping of the waters, and out-
bursting of the moon, I awoke.'

Professor Wilson (1785-1854).

' Where once such fairies dance no grass
Doth ever grow.'   A. Cowley (1618-1667).

WILLIAM BLAKE
(Poet and Painter).

'A lovely child of Wealthy parents was one day
brought to Blake. Sitting in his old worn clothes,
amidst poverty, decent indeed, but only one degree
above absolute bareness, he looked at her very
kindly for a long while without speaking, and then
gently stroking her head, and long bright curls, said,
"May God make this world to you, my child, as
beautiful as it has been to me ! " '   Francis T. Palgrave,

WILLIAM BLAKE'S 'SONGS OF INNOCENCE.'

' The lovely and luminous setting of designs, which
makes the songs precious and pleasurable to those
who know or care for little else of the master's doing,
the infinite delight of those drawings, sweeter to see
than music to hear, where herb and stem break into
grace of shape and blossom of form, and the branch
work is full of little flames and flowers, catching as it
were from the verse enclosed the fragrant heat and deli-

cate sound they seem to give back, where colour lapses
into light, and light assumes feature in colour. If elsewhere the artist's strange strength of thought and hand
is more visible, nowhere is there such pure sweetness
and singleness of design in his work. All the tremulous
and tender splendour of Spring is mixed with the
written word and coloured draught. Every page has
the smell of April, over all things given—the sleep of
flocks, and the growth of leaves, the laughter in divid-
ing lips of flowers, and the music of the moulded mouth
of the flute-player—there is cast a pure fine veil of
light, softer than sleep and keener than sunshine.'

A. C. Swinburne.

.*. This is a very eloquent and a very truthful tribute
to the Songs of Innocence, I entirely agree with it.
Yet I do not know any man of genius who is more
often unreadable in his writings, and more repellent in a
great many of his designs, than Blake.

MATRIMONY.

'There lived a carle on Kellyburnbraes' who had a
considerable grudge against marriage, and no wonder,
but, to my mind, though matrimony may be a homely,
at any rate, it is a respectable, and, I may safely say, a
necessary condition of existence, and everybody, time
being given them, at last comes round to this opinion.
Let me instance that noble creature Mary Wollstone-

craft (among women) and her gifted son-in-law (among men),—but they were slow to find it out.

It has been often asserted that if Chancellor Cairns had the arrangement of all our marriages (his own, of course, not included) there would be quite as many happy ones as at present, and certainly fewer that are simply deplorable. It strikes me, however, that such an interference is not necessary, for the component parts of all the wedded couples I happen to know seem to get on fairly well with each other; though I admit that in one or two cases she may have married him for his money, and that in another he was fascinated by her face. I lately heard of one very blessed union where the gentleman proposed because the lady exactly harmonised with his drawing-room draperies, but then that gentleman was a Fine-Art Connoisseur.

> How they loved,
> Witness, ye days and nights, and all ye hours
> That danced away with down upon your feet.

And yet everyone knows that the holy estate has its drawbacks ! We have all pretty well made up our minds on that subject. Hark to the wretch ! how playfully he sings about it !

> We are scratched, or we are bitten
> By the pets to whom we cling ;
> Oh, my Love she is a kitten,
> And my heart 's a ball of string.

And then this is a woman's advice to a woman :

> *Prenez à dextre, et à senestre—n'épargnez homme, je vous prie.*

A lady once wrote to Prince Talleyrand, that heartless nobleman, who found his pleasure between double-dealing at Downing Street and short whist at the Travellers', informing him, in high-flown terms of grief, of the death of her husband. She expected an eloquent answer of condolence, and this is what she got: 'Hélas! madame, votre affectionné &c. &c., Talleyrand.'

In less than a year another letter, from the same lady, informed the Prince that she had married again. To which he returned an equally curt response, as follows : 'Oh, ho ! madame, votre affectionné &c. &c., Talleyrand.'

But is there not something to be said for second marriages ? It is not merely pouring hot water on the used tea-leaves. Surely not. And speaking of second marriages, I have a queer story for you. Have you ever been in Scotland ? If so, you may have noticed that the bereaved ones often continue to wear 'weepers' (those blowsy symbols of woe) long after the funeral is past and over. One is always coming across people with this outrageous decoration, it streams from their hats, or reposes between their shoulders, as they hurry along intent on their every-day avocations.

Dear ladies, this is my story. A gentleman left his home, heart-broken for the loss of his young wife. He fled abroad—he remained there. He was never

heard of, though there was a vague rumour that he had
been seen somewhere in the Valley of the Euphrates,
or some such unlikely locality. All his friends were
distressed for him. Several months elapsed, and at last
a letter arrived from him to say that he was in England,
that he would be at home immediately, and that he
would bring a new wife with him. Here was a sur-
prise! There was no time for preparation, but his
faithful old housekeeper did what she could, and
by a great effort she succeeded in getting rid of
everything that could possibly remind him of his
terrible loss.

The old house was made as cheery as possible.

The day arrived, the carriage drove up, the bride
descended. She was handed out by her husband.
He still wore the hat he had carried at his first wife's
funeral, and the *weeper* was still hanging from it!
This Scot, to say the least of it, had an imperfect
appreciation of the fitness of things.

Here is another Scottish story. It may be called
a Drawback.

A lady went to call on a young woman who had
been in her service, and who had got married. The
girl was out, but she saw her mother, who did the
honours, showing her over the house, which was very
neat, and clean, and comfortable; and the lady said,
'Really, how very nice, I am sure Fanny must be very
happy;' to which the mother replied, 'Ou, ay, but

there's joost ane little drâback.' She was shown the garden ; the same remark was made, and the same reply; and then the poultry-house, &c., and again the same reply. On which the lady very naturally said, ' But if your daughter has such an exceedingly nice home, and is so *very* comfortable, what, may I ask, is this drawback you speak of ?' It was then that the mother spoke out, exclaiming energetically, 'SHE CANNA BIDE HER MARN ! '

Here is even a queerer story, this time of a widow, perhaps the same lady after she was quit of her encumbrance.

A lady in a widow's cap, and possessed of a certain amount of fascination, startled a gentleman in whose company she was unexpectedly thrown, by bursting into tears. 'Why do you weep, madam?' politely asked the gentleman. 'Oh, sir,' replied the lady, gazing at him through her tears, 'you do so remind me of my poor dear husband.' Upon the gentleman inquiring with still politer, and, perhaps, warmer sympathy, ' Dear madam, am I then so very like him ? ' she replied, with a fresh gush of weeping, ' Oh, dear, no, sir, it is because you are the' very *hopposite* of him.'

This was Thomas Fuller's notion of what a good wife should be : ' She is none of your dainty dames who love to appear in a variety of suits, every day new ; but *our* good wife sets up a sail according to the keel of her husband's estate, and, if of high parentage, she does not so remember what she was by birth, that she forgets what she is by match.'

One word more,—I have a well-considered opinion as to the proper ages for man and wife. A wife should be half the age of her husband *with seven years added.* Thus, if the gentleman is twenty, his wife should be seventeen. If he is thirty-six, she should be twenty-five; and so on. No lady of the ripe age of fifty-seven has a right to indulge in the luxury of a spouse who (even though he may not be a magnificent ruin) is less than a century.

BARLEY BROTH.

(Cumberland Dialect.)

' If tempers were put up to seale,
    Our Jwohn's wad bear a duced preyce ;
He vow'd 'twas barley i' the broth,—
    " Upon my word," says I, " it's reyce."

' " I mek nea faut," our Jwohnny says,
    " The broth is guid and varra neyce ;
I only say—it's barley broth."
    " You says what's wrang," says I, " it's reyce."

' " Did ever mortal hear the leyke !
As if I hadn't sense to tell !
Tou may think reyce the better thing,
But barley broth dis just as well."

' " And say is mud, if it was there ;
The deil a grain is i' the pot ;
But tou mun ayways threep yen down,—
I've drawn the deevil of a lot ! "

' " And what's the lot that I have drawn?
Pervarsion is a woman's neame !
Sae fares-te-weel ! I'll sarve my King,
And never, never, mair come heame."

' Now Jenny frets frae mworn to neet ;
The Sunday cap's nae longer neyce !
She aye puts barley i' the broth,
And hates the varra neame o' reyce.

' Thus treyfles vex, and treyfles please,
And treyfles mek the sum o' leyfe ;
And treyfles mek a bonny lass
A wretched or a happy weyfe !'

Susanna Blamire (1747-1794).

.*. This lady's Poems were collected and published
in 1842 ; some of them are well worth reading. This
is by no means the best of them.

A RUSTIC LOVE-LETTER.

' Dear John,' the letter ran, ' it can't, can't be,—
  For father's gone to Chorley Fair with Sam,
And mother's storing apples.   Prue and me
  Up to our elbows making damson jam:
But we shall meet before a week is gone,
'Tis a long lane that has no turning, John.

' Only till Sunday next, and then you'll wait
  Behind the white thorn, by the broken stile,
We can go round, and catch them at the gate,
  All by ourselves, for nearly one long mile.
Dear Prue won't look, and father he'll go on,
And Sam's two eyes are all for Cissy, John.

' John, she's so smart ; with every ribbon new,
  Flame-coloured sac, and crimson Padesoy,
As proud as proud, and has the vapours too,
  Just like my lady ! calls poor Sam a boy,
And vows no sweetheart's worth the thinking on
Till he's past thirty.   I know better, John.

' My dear, I don't think that I thought of much
  Before we knew each other, I and you ;
And now, why, John, your least, least finger touch
  Gives me enough to think a summer through.
See, for I send you something ! there, 'tis gone !
Look in this corner ; mind you find it, John.'

Austin Dobson.

.*. Surely these are very happy stanzas, simple and not flat, tender and not sentimental. I see no reason why they should not be as acceptable fifty years hence as they are to-day, but certainly fifty years is a long time !

SWISS MOUNTAINS.

'I well recollect the walk on the winding road from Sallenche, sloping up the hills towards St.-Gervais, one cloudless Sunday afternoon. The road circles softly between bits of rocky bank and mounded pasture, little cottages and chapels gleaming out from among the trees at every turn. Behind me, some leagues in length, rose the jagged range of the mountains of the Réposoir ; on the other side of the valley, the mass of the Aiguille de Varens, heaving its seven thousand feet of cliff into the air at a single effort, its gentle gift of waterfall, the Nant d'Arpenaz, like a pillar of cloud at its feet ; Mont Blanc and all its aiguilles, one silver flame, in front of me : marvellous blocks of mossy granite, and dark glades of pine around me.'   John Ruskin.

A LUCKY NUMBER.

H—— tells me that his cook has lately won a good sum of money in a lottery, with the number *twenty-*

three. H—— asked her how it was she had happened to tumble on such a lucky number, and she replied, ' Oh, sir, I had a dream, I dreamt of number seven, and I dreamt it three times, and as three times seven is twenty-three, I chose that number, sir.' This proves that an ignorance of the multiplication-table is not always a calamity.

I was relating this anecdote to a distinguished friend, who holds rather a responsible position, and is usually anything but slow in apprehending a joke. When I had concluded, I observed a wistful expression on his countenance, as if he were ready, nay anxious, to be amused, but could not for the life of him quite manage it. Then suddenly his face brightened, and he said, but with a tinge of dejection in his manner, ' Ah, yes, I see—yes—I suppose three times seven is not twenty-three.'

EDUCATION OF THE MIND.

' There are few men whose minds are not more or less in that state of sham knowledge against which Socrates made war. There is no man whose notions have not been first got together by spontaneous, unexamined, unconscious, uncertified association, resting upon forgotten particulars, blending together disparates or inconsistencies, and leaving in his mind old and familiar phrases, and oracular propositions, of which he has never rendered to himself account. There is no man who, if he be destined for vigorous and profitable scientific effort, has not found it a necessary branch of self-education to break up, disentangle, analyse, and reconstruct these ancient mental compounds, and who has not been driven to do it by his own lame and solitary efforts, since the giant of the Colloquial Elenchus no longer stands in the market-place to lend him help and stimulus.'

George Grote.

DOOMSDAY BOOK.

I have heard that while the Houses of Parliament were burning, the then Dean of Westminster (Ireland) stood on the leads of the Chapter-house with Sir Francis Palgrave, and they saw the fire rapidly approaching them. Sir F. Palgrave suggested that they should run and secure Doomsday Book, &c. &c., and place them somewhere in safety, but Dean Ireland assured him it would not be possible to do so without an order from the First Lord of the Treasury.

AMERICAN RESTAURANTS.

In American places of refreshment, where time is precious, and everybody is in a desperate hurry, the people bolt their food at a furious rate, and if you stop for only one instant, the waiter comes up close to you, and says quickly, and curtly, in your ear, 'Are you through?' (Have you finished?) At one of these places a hungry man broke his tooth with a large iron nail that had been served in the dish, and showed it to the waiter with an injured air. 'Wall,' said the man, looking equally injured, 'What did *you* expect? *You* didn't expect, did you, to find a silk umbrella in a ten cent hash!'

THE GREENLANDERS' HEAVEN.

The poor Greenlanders fear that the Christian Heaven will not be altogether satisfactory to them, because the missionaries, very unwisely, and certainly very unwarrantably, tell them that there are no seals in Heaven.

A HAPPY RETORT.

I am told that a certain friend of mine, as an undergraduate at Cambridge, was of an extreme nimbleness, an agility which he could not well control. One day that grave and reverend personage, the Master of his college, happening to meet him, remonstrated with him thus: 'Mr. Dash, I am sorry to say I never look out of my window but I see you jumping over those railings.' Mr. Dash was equal to the emergency, for he respectfully replied, 'And it is a curious fact, sir, that I never leap over those railings without seeing you looking out of that window.'

Mr. Dash now confines his nimbleness to metrical exercises. He is still a wag, and, what is more, he is champion of our Lyrical Light Weights.

THE TIGHT BOOTS.

'My boots are tight : the hour is late ;
My faltering footsteps deviate :
And through the stillness of the night
A wail is heard—"My boots are tight!"

'O weary hour ! O wretched woe !
It's only half-past three, or so.
We've not had much ; I feel all right,
Except my boots ; they're *very* tight.

'Old friend ! I love you more and more,
Though we have met but once before.
Since then I've had a deal of sorrow ;—
You'll come and dine with me to-morrow ?

'What's this ? A tear ? I do not think
You gave us half enough to drink.
The moon up there looks precious queer,
She's winking. Ha ! Another tear !

'I'm not a man who courts a row,
But you insulted me, just now.
By *Jove*, my friend, for what you've said,
I've half a mind to punch your head.

'You won't forget to-morrow, eh?
I'm sure to be at home all day.
Policeman, have you got a light?
Thanks.   Yes, they *are*, as you say, tight.

'The man I like's the sort of man
A man can trust, you un'erstan'.
I call that man a man, you know:
He *is* a man.   Precisely so.

'If any man addresses me,
No matter who that man may be;
I always say, 'twixt man and man,
This man's a *man*—you un'erstan

'The houses have a quivering look.
That corner one distinctly shook;
I've got another fellow's hat;
Well, never mind! all's one for that.

The gas goes leaping up and down,
We can't be right for Camden Town.
This road went east the other-day;
I think south-west's a shorter way.

'There used to be a place near here
Where one could get a glass of beer.
I wish we had some bottled Bass—
What *is* the matter with the gas?

'There's hardly wind enough to blow
The reedy lamp-posts to and fro :
And yet you see how each one leans—
I wonder what the deuce it means?

'My pipe's gone out: the air is chill;
Is this Mile End or Maida Hill?
Remember—six o'clock we dine :
Bring several friends—say eight or nine.

'The tavern bar was warm and bright,
And cheerful with a ruddy light.
Let's go back there and stop all night ;—
I can't walk home : my boots are tight.'

'Fun.'

DISTINCTION.

'Not drunk is he who from the floor
Can rise alone, and still drink more ;
But drunk is he who prostrate lies,
Without the power to drink or rise.'

GHOSTS.

' Ghost stories are absurd. Whenever a real ghost appears, by which I mean some man or woman dressed up to frighten another, if the supernatural character of the apparition has been for an instant believed, the effect on the spectator has always been most terrible. Convulsions, madness, idiocy, or even death on the spot ; but in our common ghost stories you always find that the seer, after a most appalling apparition, as you are led to believe, is quite well the next day ! This shows that the apparition was the creature of his own mind.'   Samuel T. Coleridge (1772–1834).

JOHN WICKLIFFE.

' It was to the schism in the Papacy that Wickliffe was probably indebted for permission to end his turbulent life in peace, in his own parish, and in his own bed. The real disposition of Rome towards this arch-heretic was sufficiently testified when, forty-one years afterwards, the Council of Constance, in impotent rage, condemned his bones to be exhumed, burnt, and cast into the brook. But the Swift, such is its name, bore them to the Avon, that to the Severn, the Severn to the sea, to be dispersed unto all lands—which things are an allegory.'   Thomas Fuller.

En virtutem mortis nesciam.
Vivet Lancinus Curtius
　　Sæcula per omnia
Quascunque lustrans oras,
Tantum possunt Camœnæ.

QUANTITY v. *QUALITY.*

' One of the strangest parts of Pagan worship in the East is the Mani, or praying machine. The deities are believed to be operated upon by the *number* of prayers, and as the 'devout cannot say them fast enough, a wheel is used, which enormously accelerates the process. In this way a man may sit talking of ordinary subjects to his friend while turning the wheel which repeats his prayers.

' In public places in Japan wheels with three spokes are benevolently mounted on stout posts for the gratuitous use of travellers. In a Buddhist monastery at Lahore there are about thirty wheels arranged along a gallery, capable of being moved at the slightest touch. Our guide ran his hand along the wall, setting all the wheels in motion, and thus, in one minute, saying, by proxy, more prayers than, by the ordinary method, he could get through in a day. There was a wheel outside the monastery, situate on the banks of a small stream, and, by a cog-wheel underneath, it was kept in perpetual praying motion by the water.

'The Maori have a string attached to their idols; the worshipper sits on a praying stone, at a little distance, holding in his hand the flax cord which is fastened about the idol's neck. Every now and again he gives it a jerk to make quite sure that the idol is not disregarding his petitions.'

'Day of Rest,' Aug. 1, 1876.

A FUNERAL SERMON.

A clergyman, an original, preached a funeral discourse on the beloved Princess Charlotte of Wales, and chose for his text : 'Go, see now this cursed woman, and bury her, for she is a king's daughter.' After this sufficiently startling keynote, he began his sermon : 'If this was said of Jezebel, what honour should not be paid to one who was so virtuous, and so well beloved?' &c., &c.

GUSTO.

'Gusto in art is power or passion defining any object. There is gusto in the colouring of Titian ; not only do his heads seem to think, his bodies seem to feel. This is what the Italians mean by the morbidezza of his flesh-colour. It seems sensitive and alive all over, not merely to have the look and texture of flesh, but the feeling in itself. For example, the limbs of his female figures have a luxurious softness and delicacy which appears conscious of the pleasure of the beholder. As the objects themselves in nature would produce an impression on the sense, distinct from every other object, and having something divine in it which the heart owns, and the imagination consecrates, the objects of the picture preserve the same impression, absolute, unimpaired, stamped with all the truth of passion, the pride of the eye, and the charm of beauty. Rubens makes his flesh-colour like flowers. Titian's is like flesh, and like nothing else. It is as different from that of other painters as the skin is from a piece of white or red drapery thrown over it. The blood circulates here and there, the blue veins just appear, the rest is distinguished throughout only by that sort of tingling sensation to the eye which the body feels within itself. This is gusto. Again, Titian's landscapes have a prodigious gusto, both in the colouring and in the forms. We shall never forget one we saw many years ago in the Orleans Gallery, of Actæon hunting. It had a brown, mellowed, autumnal look. The sky was of the colour of stone. The winds seemed to sing through the rustling branches of the trees, and already you might hear the twanging of bows resound through the tangled mazes of the wood.

' Rubens has a great deal of gusto in his fauns and

satyrs, and in all that expresses motion, but in nothing else. Rembrandt has it in everything; everything in his pictures has a tangible character. There is gusto in Pope's compliments, in Dryden's satires, and Prior's tales. "The Beggar's Opera" is full of it.'

William Hazlitt (1778–1830).

NOTHING.

What the contented man desires—
The poor man has, the rich requires—
The miser gives, the spendthrift saves,
And all men carry to their graves.

MILESIAN HUMOUR.

There was a row in the gallery of a Dublin theatre. a scuffle, and one voice shouted, 'Turn him out;' another, 'Throw him over.' 'Ay,' added a third, a very bloodthirsty Milesian, 'and don't waste him, boys—kill a fiddler with him.'

TO A PROUD KINSWOMAN.

Fair maid, had I not heard thy baby cries,
Nor seen thy girlish sweet vicissitude,
Thy mazy motions, striving to elude

Yet wooing still a parent's watchful eyes,
Thy humours, many as the opal's dyes,
   And lovely all : methinks thy scornful mood,—
   And bearing high of stately womanhood,
Thy brow where beauty sits to tyrannize
O'er humble love, had made me sadly fear thee;
   For never, sure, was seen a Royal Bride ·
   Whose gentleness gave grace to so much pride.
My very thoughts would tremble to be near thee.
   But when I see thee at thy father's side,
Old times unqueen thee, and old loves endear thee.'

Hartley Coleridge (1796–1849).

RHYME.

Seven or eight years ago an amusing controversy was held in the ' Graphic,' between Messrs. Burnand and Gilbert, that captivating pair! on the subject of Rhyme, and not without reason too, for there is no doubt that, at present, the English rhymer has an uncommon hard time of it.

There are some quite common words which have no rhyme at all, and which ought to have one, and there are others which have only one or two rhymes, and which ought to have more.

To lessen this difficulty, a difficulty which troubled Milton, and which now encourages a large number of otherwise well-behaved people to take refuge in, what they are pleased to call, Milton's blank verse, Mr. Gilbert ingeniously suggested that as inventors, often gave arbitrary and irrational names to their inventions, they might become still further public benefactors, if hereafter in selecting these names they would have an eye to enriching our language with rhymes to words which at present are rhymeless. Such, for instance, as 'silver,' and 'month;' and he added something to this effect, that if only the mechanist had been still more ingenious, and had called his invention a '*Chilver*,' and the chemist had christened his discovery a '*Ronth*,' there would not have been the necessity for such a controversy.

I agree with Mr. Gilbert, but I am inclined to go further. Why should not the Poet-Laureate, and Mr. Gilbert, and Mr. Burnand, and the other sons of song, agree, in conclave, to select, say a couple of dozen words (I would limit them to a couple of dozen or so) as rhymes to parts of speech which, at present, have either no rhyme at all, or only one or two? *Anguish*, for instance, has not it been long enough doomed to *languish* for a fresh echo to itself; and is not it annoying that when we mention the one, our readers know that the other is not far off? When once these words have been selected, their exact significance can be decided upon; and, after that, there should be no power of appeal.

To give an idea of what I propose, it might be
determined that a new word, *lupid* for instance, should
hereafter, and for all time, represent the crescent-moon
(the crescent-moon is useful in poetry). *Ranguish*, for
the same reason, might signify a half-blown rose.
And could not a *pladow* do duty for a blonde beauty,
and a *graiden* for a brunette? A few such words, well
chosen, would be an immense boon on the slopes of
Parnassus,—a boon to all the poets, excepting Mr.
Browning, who finds an echo to every part of speech
in the language, and as many as he desires.

ABSENCE OF MIND.

'Some people like lizards, but there is too much
affectation about the lizard to make him altogether
admirable. In the first place, his laborious assump-
tion of a thoughtful demeanour. Pretending to be
abstracted in deepest cogitation, he will remain motionless on your wall for the hour together; and I
deny, with "Christopher North," that any man has a
right "to leave his carcase in a room without the mind"
(or without appearing to have the mind) "that belongs
to it."'   Mr. P. Robinson's 'In My Indian Garden.'

.*. It had occurred to me that lizards might be

listening intently—sensible to sounds altogether in-
audible to our dull ears.   How well Bernard Palissy has
given them on his quaint reptile dishes: to say nothing
of the bronze paper-weights to be bought in Rome.

A landed proprietor, a kind and sympathizing
person, but at the same time curiously absent-minded,
called on a tenant to condole on the death of a
valuable cow—a very valuable cow.   The cause of
the misfortune had been enveloped in mystery.   The
farmer began a long-winded history of the untoward
event, his landlord soon going off into the clouds.   The
last words of the narrative were, ' And, can you believe
it, my Lord ? when we opened her, we found she had
been choked by a large turnip that was sticking in her
gullet.'   At this point the sympathetic but absent-
minded landlord woke up, and said, in rather a con-
gratulatory tone of voice too, ' Ah, yes, and so you got
your turnip.'

Speaking of absence of mind, Samuel Rogers said
that his old friend Maltby, the brother of the Bishop,
was a very absent man.   ' One day at Paris, in the
Louvre, we were looking at the pictures, when a lady
entered who spoke to me, and kept me some minutes
in conversation.   On rejoining Maltby, I said, " That
was Mrs. —— ; we had not met for so long that she had
almost forgotten me, and asked me if my name was

"Rogers." Maltby, still looking at the pictures, said, "And was it?'"

A certain old Scottish divine was singularly absent-minded. One day strolling with a pupil in the fields near Edinburgh, and reading a book, he walked up against a cow that was grazing. He took off his hat to the animal and said, gravely, 'I beg your pardon, madam.' The pupil said, 'It is not a lady, sir, it is a cow.' The next day he was in Princes Street, and happened to come against a lady, and immediately exclaimed, 'Ah, there you are again, you beast.'

A hospitable but absent-minded gentleman was dining out where the dinner was anything but good, and for the moment, forgetting where he was, and fancying he was in his own house, he began to apologize for the wretchedness of the repast.

————

SCOTTISH METAPHYSICS.

Sydney Smith said that he overheard a young lady of his acquaintance, at a dance in Edinburgh, exclaim in a sudden pause of the music, 'What you say, my lord, is very true of love *in the aibstract*, but——' Here the fiddlers began fiddling furiously, and the rest was lost.

You see the Scots are very metaphysical. They even make love metaphysically! It was the Rev. S. Smith who furnished the following definition :—

'When one man is talking to another, who does not understand him, and when he that is talking does not understand himself, why, you know, *these* are metaphysics.'

———◆◇◆———

JEREMY TAYLOR TO JOHN EVELYN.

'Dear Sir,—I am in some disorder by reason of the death of a little child of mine. A boy that lately made us very glad, but now he rejoices in his little orbe, while we sigh, and think, and long to be as safe as he is.'

———◆◇◆———

INFANCY.

'The human infant is a picture of such deformity, weakness, nakedness, and helpless distress, as is not to be found among the home-born animals of this world. The chicken has its birth from no sin, and therefore comes forth in beauty; it runs and pecks as soon as its shell is broken. The calf and the lamb go both to play as soon as the dam is delivered of them. They are pleased with themselves, and please the eye that beholds their frolicsome state and beauteous clothing ; whilst the babe newly born of a woman, that is to have an upright form, and view the heavens, and worship the God that made it, lies for months in gross ignorance, weakness, and impurity, as sad a spectacle when he first breathes the life of this world, as when, in the agonies of death, he breathes his last.'

Thomas à Kempis (:380-1471).

A SLEEPLESS NIGHT.

A young fellow, an Irishman, in the Marshalsea prison, the last thing, as he dropt off to sleep at night, having seen his companion brushing his teeth, and then, on awaking in the morning, seeing him again at the same work, exclaimed 'Och, a weary night ye must have had of it, Mr. Fitzgerald.'

ATHEISM.

'The Emperor Tiberius was one of the ablest men who ever sat on a throne. His State Papers, if we may use the term, are singularly luminous and masterly. Yet it was the Emperor Tiberius, the world's undisputed master, who thus wrote to the Senate :—" May all the gods and goddesses, if there be any, damn me worse than I am damned already, if I know what to write to you." '

'The Atheistic Life,' by Rev. T. B. Brown.

I quote this passage in ignorance of the context, but, it is quite possible that Tiberius may have written in a moment of extreme irritability or depression ; such as might be occasioned by even a passing ailment.

THE MAID OF ATHENS.

An admirer of Lord Byron wrote to Mrs. Black (the 'Maid of Athens'), after she had grown old, for her autograph, and a lock of her 'tresses unconfined,' with neither of which requests she could possibly comply, as she had never learnt to write, and had no hair left.

AUTOGRAPHS.

There are a good many autograph books, and there are autographs of many different kinds—Mr. Thomas Hood describes several of them ; of one he says :—'A friend of mine possesses an autograph— "REMEMBER JIM HOSKINS"—done with a red-hot poker on the back kitchen door'—and then he adds : ' This, however, is an awkward autograph *to bind up.*' .

ITALY.

'We are accustomed to hear the South of Italy spoken of as a beautiful country; its mountain forms are graceful above others, its sea bays exquisite in outline and hue ; but it is only beautiful in superficial aspect. In closer detail it is wild and melancholy. Its forests are sombre-leaved, labyrinth-stemmed ; the carubbe, the olive, laurel, and ilex are alike in that strange feverish twisting of their branches, as if in, spasms of half-human pain. Avernus forests ; one fears to break their boughs, lest they should cry to us from the rents : the rocks they shade are of ashes, or thrice-molten lava : iron sponge, whose every pore has been filled with fire. Silent villages, earthquake-shaken, without commerce, without industry, without knowledge, without hope, gleam in white ruin from hill-side to hillside ; far-winding wrecks of immemorial walls surround the dust of cities long forsaken ; the mountain streams moan through the cold arches of their foundations, green with weed, and rage over the heaps of their fallen towers. Far above, in thunder-blue serration, stand the eternal edges of the angry Apennine, dark with rolling impendence of volcanic cloud.'
John Ruskin.

PICTURE POEMS FOR YOUNG FOLKS.

' Is the yellow bird dead ?
Lay your dear little head
Close, close to my heart, and weep, precious one,
        there :
' While your beautiful hair
On my bosom lies light, like a sun-lighted cloud ;
    No, you need not keep still,
    You may sob as you will ;
There is some little comfort in crying aloud.

' But the days they must come
When your grief will be dumb :
Grown women, like me, must take care how they cry,
    You will learn, by-and-bye ;
'Tis a womanly art to hide pain out of sight,
    To look round with a smile,
    Tho' your heart aches the while,
And to keep back your tears till you've blown out the
        light.'

Marian Douglas.

TALL TALKING.

A gentleman from Kentucky boasted that he could
' jump higher, *and stay up longer*—dive deeper, *and
come up dryer*—than any other man in Kentuck.'

BORES.

I have a friend who is a most respectable man, and a most intolerable Bore. He is a considerable talker, but, at the same time, his conversation is curiously elementary : he will tell you, and half a dozen times over for that matter, that coalscuttles are hard and that feather-beds are soft, and he will get quite excited about it.

Then he is a moralist : he has quite made up his— what shall we call it?—his mind that honesty is the best policy : he is a sagacious man too—a man of the world—for he maintains, earnestly—strenuously (he takes off his coat to it, as it were) that a bird in the hand is worth two birds in the bush : and he does so as if he were in the process of making the discovery. It is impossible to get a fresh idea into his head; you try to do so, and you feel you might quite as well play jigs to a milestone. A young friend, who chanced to be in a cynical mood, remarked of him that his talk was as dull as ditch water, without the animalculæ. People complain of Club Bores and such like, but what are Club Bores? You need not go to your Club, but *here* he is. Yes, commend me to your *domestic* Bore! —that being who walks in with the breakfast urn, and only leaves you with his flat candlestick.

My brother ! have *you* ever been afflicted by a Bore? If so, go forth, refresh yourself with Charles

I

Dickens' essay on ·the species, and you will feel the better for it. Among many other pleasant things he says : ' Our Bore is admitted on all hands to be a good-hearted man. He may put fifty people out of temper, but he keeps his own. He preserves a sickly, stolid smile upon his face when other faces are ruffled by the perfection he has attained in his art, and has an equable voice which never travels out of one key, or rises above one pitch. His manner is a manner of tranquil interest. None of his opinions are startling. Among his deepest rooted convictions, it may be mentioned that he considers the air of England damp, and holds that our lively neighbours—he always calls the French our lively neighbours—have the advantage of us in that particular. Nevertheless, he is unable to forget ' that John Bull is John Bull all the world over, and that England with all her faults is England still.' . . .

Do you remember what Ben Jonson said about Bores? He said ' a tedious person is one a man would leap a steeple from.' But there are worse people than Bores. Commend me, I say, to your regular *Old Man of the Sea*, who may be spiteful, or conceited, or con-sequential, as well as prosy, and perhaps all four. ' Some men have souls so dull and stupid that they serve for little else than to keep their bodies from putrefaction.'

I only wish we could treat our Bores as we treat our worst criminals—quench them for the public good ;

and I do not see why we should not do so. Surely there is such a thing as Free Will. The malefactor, whether he belong to a low type of humanity or not, and a good many belong to a very low type indeed, ought to have known better; he has committed murder, it is his own fault, and he must be held responsible. String him up! Even supposing there is no such thing as Free Will, surely we should be equally justified. The Bore might, and probably would, in a stolid, boring sort of way, remonstrate that he could not help it, but our reply would be, 'You have bored us to death, you waste our time, your opinions are antiquated, you converse prosily on previously exhausted subjects, you wear your hearers out, and you are altogether unendurable—you are of no use to anybody, and the comfort of the public is of more importance than the very limited chance of your moral renovation. You offend because you cannot help offending—we shall punish you because we cannot help punishing. Our aim is the public good—STRING HIM UP!

RICHARD B. SHERIDAN.

(1751—1816).

By all accounts R. B. Sheridan must have been a delightfully easy-going fellow. I have heard that Mr. and Mrs. Creevy happened to be dining with the

Sheridans, and, after dinner, Sheridan seemed preoc-
cupied; and when Creevy rallied him about it, Sheridan
said, 'The fact is, Creevy, that just before your carriage
drove up to our door a letter had arrived, acquainting
Mrs. Sheridan and me that a sum of money had been
left us. We had just time to agree, solemnly agree,
that we would not breathe a syllable about it to anyone; and it is only my certain and entire conviction
that Mrs. Sheridan upstairs is at this moment telling
the good news to Mrs. Creevy which justifies me in
telling it to you down here.' On another occasion
Sheridan was rather bored by the society of a lady
who wished to go out walking with him; but a lucky
shower of rain coming on, they were obliged to remain
in doors, so he escaped the infliction. After a short
time, however, it began to clear up, and Sheridan
stole to the door to escape; on this the lady also got
up, saying, 'Ah, I see there's a little blue sky now.'
'Yes, there is,' said Sheridan; 'enough for one, but not
enough for two.'

REGRET.

'Mild is the parting year, and sweet
　The odour of the falling spray;
Life passes on more rudely fleet,
　And balmless is its closing day.

I wait its close, I court its gloom,
But mourn that never must there fall ·
Or on my breast or on my tomb
The tear that would have sooth'd it all.'

W. S. Landor (1775—1864).

A PORTRAIT BY VELASQUEZ.

'A dwarf seated in a heap on the ground, with a ·
book on his knee, and an inkstand at his feet.

'There were differences among Philip's dwarfs
which Velasquez perceived with his keen, artistic intelligence, and profound observation of mankind ; one
of them was merely silly, another scowled hatred and
envy from under his beetling brows, but this one whose
image is here before us bears the pain of a nobler suffering. O, sad and thoughtful face, looking out upon us
from the serious canvas of Velasquez, though the grave
has closed upon thee for two hundred years, we know
what were thy miseries ! To be the butt of idle princes
and courtiers, and, worse than that, to be treated by the
most beautiful women as a thing that could have no
passion, to be admitted to an intimacy which was but
the negation of thy manhood, to have ridicule for thy
portion, and buffoonery for thy vocation, and yet to be
at the same time fully conscious of an inward human
dignity, continually outraged, of a capacity for learning
and for thought !'   Mr. Philip G. Hamerton.

'Railing at a man for his bodily infirmities is like beating a cripple with his own crutches.'

Thomas Fuller.

PLEAD FOR ME.

'Stern Reason is to judgment come,
  Array'd in all her forms of gloom;
  Wilt thou, my advocate, be dumb?
    No, radiant angel, speak and say
    Why I did cast the world away.

'Why I have persevered to shun
  The common path that others run,
  And on a strange road journeyed on,
    Heedless alike of wealth and power,
    Of glory's crown and pleasure's flower.

'These once indeed seemed Beings Divine;
  And they, perchance, heard vows of mine,
  And saw my offerings on their shrine;
    But careless gifts are seldom prized,
    And mine were worthily despised.

'So with a weary heart I swore
  To seek their altar-stone no more;
  And gave my spirit to adore
    Thee, ever present, phantom-thing;
    My slave, my comrade, and my King!

Emily Brontë (1818—1848).

FAMILY PRAYERS.

Lady P—— used to tell a story of a household who were pious and proper, and had rather an absurd way of showing it. After prayers the male servants left the dining-room by one door, and the female servants by another. 'But, you know,' added she, 'when they got to the bottoms of their respective staircases' (which met) 'the kissin' was like the crackin' o' whips.' Lady P—— lisped, which made the story funnier.

SOCIETY IN LONDON.

A distinguished diplomatist from the United States of America, a very genial and social being, soon after his arrival in London made the round of the sights, Madame Tussaud's among the number. 'And what do you think of our wax-work?' said a friend. 'Well,' replied the General, 'it struck me as being very like any ordinary English party.'

UNBECOMING CURIOSITY.

A tradesman, to whom Talleyrand was indebted a considerable sum, having made many unsuccessful efforts to obtain payment, planted himself in the *porte cochère* of the Prince's hotel, and resolutely accosted him as he was entering his carriage. 'Que me voulez-vous, monsieur?' asked the minister. 'Monsieur, je veux seulement savoir *quand* son Excellence voudrait bien me payer?' 'Vous êtes bien curieux,' observed his Excellency, pulling up the window.

----♦----

NATURE.

'I don't know anything sweeter than this leaking in of Nature through all the cracks in the walls and floors of cities. You heap up a million tons of hewn rocks on a square mile or two of earth which was green once. The trees look down from the hill-sides and ask each other, as they stand on tiptoe—"What are these people about?" And the small herbs at their feet look up and whisper back—"We will go and see." Then the wind steals to them at night, and they go softly with it into the great city,—one to a cleft in the pavement, one to a spout on the roof, one to a seam in the marbles over a rich gentleman's bones, and one to a grave without a stone where nothing but a man is buried,—and there they grow, looking down on the generations of men from mouldy roofs, looking up from between the less-trodden pavements, looking out through iron cemetery-railings.

'Listen to them, when there is only a light breath stirring, and you will hear them saying to each other—.

"Wait awhile!" The words run along the telegraph of those narrow green lines that border the roads leading from the city, until they reach the slope of the hills, and the trees repeat in low murmurs to each other,—"Wait awhile!"

'By-and-by the flow of life in the streets ebbs, and the old leafy inhabitants, the smaller tribes always in front—saunter in, one by one, very careless seemingly, but very tenacious, until they swarm so that the great stones gape from each other with the crowding of their roots, and the feldspar begins to be picked out of the granite to find them food. At last the trees take up their solemn line of march, and never rest until they have encamped in the market-place. Wait long enough and you will find an old doting oak hugging a huge worn block in its yellow underground arms; that was the corner-stone of the State House. O, so patient She is, this imperturbable Nature!'

Dr. O. W. Holmes.

A LIVELY CHEESE.

At a friend's house Charles Lamb was presented with a cheese; it was a very ripe, not to say a very *lively* cheese, and, as Lamb was leaving, his friend offered him a piece of paper in which to wrap it, so that he might convey it more conveniently. 'Thank you,' said Charles, ' but would not several yards of twine be better, and then, you know I could *lead* it home ? '

———◦◇◦———

MR. SAMUEL ROGERS SITTING FOR HIS PORTRAIT.

It is said that Mr. Rogers once asked the Rev. Sydney Smith's advice as to the position in which he should have his portrait taken ? ' Oh,' said Sydney Smith, ' have it taken as if you were at church, in an attitude of devotion, *with your countenance in your hat.*'

It is almost needless to say that Mr. Rogers was a singularly plain person, but it is not possible that Sydney Smith ever made so unkind or ill-bred a speech to him, or anybody else.

———◦◇◦———

AN ANONYMOUS LETTER.

Mr. Thomas Raikes, who published a diary, was pitted with the small-pox, even to the tip of his nose. It seems that he wrote an anonymous, and rather offensive letter to Count D'Orsay, and as an additional insult he secured the envelope with a red wafer and stamped it with a thimble. D'Orsay guessed who was the sender, and, soon after happening to meet Raikes, he mildly counselled him thus—' The next time, *mon cher,* you write anyone an anonymous letter and would rather not be found out, do not seal it with the tip of your nose.'

———◆◇◆———

MR. WHO?

'That's empire, that which I can give away.'

Charles Lamb said the greatest pleasure he knew was to do a good action by stealth, and to have it found out by accident.

There is nothing exciting in the following paper, indeed it is prosy enough, so let no one read it unless he takes pleasure in hearing of a kindly action.

On a certain occasion, with an impulse of singular magnanimity, I had abstained from bidding against the British Museum for a little book, on the possession of which I had much set my heart. When the prize was irrevocably gone I lamented my loss, and cursed my magnanimity. I cursed it loudly and frequently, for as the volume was almost unique, there seemed to be no chance of my ever meeting with another copy. It was a book for which I had long pined, it would have exactly filled a most important gap in my slender collection ; indeed, its possession would have considerably enhanced the value of all the books on a certain short shelf. 'What,' groaned I, as Job himself might have groaned, 'what is the use

of having those other books if I haven't that particular
book?'

'That little [volume] unpossessed,
Corrodes and cankers all the rest.'

Yes, it is too provoking—' Life is a burthen.'

Some time afterwards, and by the merest accident,
. I heard of another copy of the same book; there are
not four copies known, and, strange to say, this copy
belonged to a man I knew, an opulent being, and a
collector of books. All this was disheartening, for if
he was rich, I felt sure he would be selfish ; and if he
was a collector, would he not be infinitely more selfish?
However, after pondering, I may say brooding over
the matter for some weeks, I, at last, made up my
mind.

I determined to employ an agent, one who would
have my welfare at heart. He should negotiate an
exchange, or a purchase. The agent I selected was a
very wily fellow, as sagacious as a serpent. When I
proposed my plan to him, *Il me rit au nez*, he knew
there would not be the remotest chance of my getting
the book, its possessor being himself a collector ; that
the very fact of my wishing to possess it would make
'the other party' reluctant to disgorge it. Alas ! I
feared my agent was right, for were not those exactly
my own sentiments as regarded my brother collectors ?
·However, the application was made ; and, would you
believe it, astounding as it may seem to any collector

who chances to read this little paper, the very next day my acquaintance, I may now venture to call him my friend, walked into my agent's place of business, with the book in his pocket. I ought to say that my friend is a learned man, a cultivated man, and he understood as well as I did the peculiar interest that attached to the book with which he was parting.

The title of the book is 'England's Helicon,' 1st edition, 1600, and my friend's name and address are— why may not I tell you my friend's name and address? Charles Lamb said the greatest pleasure he knew was to do a good action by stealth and to have it found out by accident. I think my friend knows a greater pleasure—he is quite satisfied to do a kindness, and then to have done with it. I know, however, he agrees with Charles Lamb in a great many things.

MR. DOO!

'On the 15th instant, at his residence in Eaton Square, deeply regretted by all who knew him, John Doo, Esquire, F.S.A., F.G.S., F.R.G.S., J.P., in the 80th year of his age. Friends are requested' &c.

Apropos of this announcement, and as a pendant to what you have just been reading, I must tell you a long history concerning another little Book, also a volume of extraordinary rarity, of which, at one time,

I very greatly coveted the possession. It had the
scarce title-page, you know, *without the date*; there is
only one other copy known with this peculiarity, and
that copy is locked up at Sion College.

This curious little book is intimately connected, in
my mind, with the above-named Mr. Doo. He·was
an old gentleman whom I frequently met at the·club.
I fancy I can see him now; he had a way of standing
before the fire with a pinch of snuff between his
fingers and the 'Art Journal' in the other hand; he
had a slow—a deliberate cough; and also a turn-up
nose, round watery eyes, with red rims, and white
hair and whiskers, and he looked for all the world
exactly like a very old bull-dog in a snow-storm. Mr.
Doo was a pompous old patron of the Fine Arts, a
person whose conversation was so empty, and so
extremely fatiguing that his fellow creatures, myself
included, gave him a wide berth, though he had once
beguiled me into going to see his pictures in Eaton
Square, and had often bored me to go and see them
again, and, as he phrased it, to 'overhaul his portfolios.'

One day, while he was holding forth on Art and
art matters generally, and the fountains in Trafalgar
Square in particular, and I was meditating how it
would be possible for me to give him the slip, he
chanced to mention the title of the rare little book at
Sion College. I instantly pricked up my ears. But

when he casually remarked that he possessed a copy
of it, I was indeed surprised, and instantly became
interested in everything concerning him—his collection—his conversation—and even his cough ! I am
ashamed, too, to confess it, but from that moment I
was more attentive to him than I had hitherto been,
I even sought him out and listened respectfully while
he bragged of his influence in the Art world ; I even
stultified myself by defending him behind his back.
And now when we talked our converse somehow
always got round to the rare little book, without the
date on the title.

One day, it was a memorable day for me, Mr. Doo
cleared his throat, and said, in his hum-drum, comfortable sort of tone, ' I have been thinking about that
shabby little old book of mine, it is tossing about
somewhere in my town house ; I begin to think it's
quite wrong for me to keep the little fellow all to
myself, I'm not worthy of such a treasure, it's much
more in your way, now,' and then he paid me one or
two rancid compliments, which I am ashamed to
detail here, and which I am more ashamed to have
half-swallowed then. ' I wish,' said he, ' you would
name a day, and come to Eaton Square, and have a
good overhauling of my portfolios,' and he added,
' and then, you know, about that book, now I really
don't think I ought to keep such an interesting little
gem all to myself. When you come I shall just put it

on the corner of the table, and you'll slip it into your
pocket as you leave, without saying anything, you
know, and that will be all about it, eh? It's quite a
gem—you know it has got the scarce title without
the date, etc.' Conceive my feelings! I at once, there
and then, fixed a day—I nailed him to it—Yes, 'to-
morrow at eleven o'clock' would suit me down to the
ground ; and the next morning, punctual to the minute,
I found myself in his library.

Of course, when I entered, I naturally looked at
all the corners of the tables—I did not see the book,
but I quite made up my mind that it would be forth-
coming at the right time, and I was cheerful, not to
say festive. We again went through all his pictures, this
time we went through them thoroughly—his Haydons,
his Hiltons, his Fuselis (all masters that I loathe), and
a smirking Romney or two—very flagrant specimens
of what may be called the '*roguish* school,' and he
had a long, long history about each, and all to his own
glorification. At length I began to grow rather weary,
a little jaded, in fact, for there was no end to the
stories, and no mention of the precious little book. At
last, to my horror, he brought out his 'folios'—*they
were a caution to snakes!* heaps and heaps of seven-
teenth-century prints, worn-out impressions after Goltzius, and the schools of M. Angelo and Rubens, the
sort of rubbish one used to see exposed for sale in
an old umbrella in the New Cut. I feigned as deep

an interest in them as I could, but my nerves were
fast giving way under all this strain. I was growing
very weary,—twelve o'clock had struck,—one o'clock
had struck,—I wish'd Old Doo at the deuce, and I began
to perceive an ominous something in his manner that
made me suspect he was beginning to have the same
sort of feeling about myself. It was close on two o'clock,
and as we turned over the last Goltzius I nearly yawned
in his face. I began to despair. I murmured something about its being ' time to go,' and of 'an appointment at the Zoological Gardens,'—I thanked him—I
spoke with effusion of his 'extreme kindness,' I begged
he would excuse me—'I must be off,—due at the monkey
house at two o'clock'—not a word about my precious
little book ! 'But you have not yet seen my folio of
Everdingen's,' said Old Doo, with a grin. 'Oh, hang
your Everdingens,' I mentally ejaculated, 'where's my
book ? '—not a word was uttered about it. I again said,
' I fear I must go,' and again I glanced at all the corners
of all the tables—I think Old Doo knew I was doing so
—we shook hands—I moved to go—I went, but as I had
my hand on the handle of the door I turned round,
and with a forced, and, I daresay, a cadaverous smile,
I said, ' By the by, Mr. Doo' (just as if it was
occurring to me now for the first time), ' I haven't seen
that little old book of yours.' ' Oh !' said Doo, in his
abominably deliberate way, ' the book, eh! Ah, yes, I've
been considering about that shabby little fellow ; yes,

K

he *is* a gem, isn't he? and really, I don't know, but the fact is, you see, I think I ought to consult my relations' (he was close on seventy years of age !) 'before I proceed further in the matter, but I've got my will to make, you know. It has the scarce title, eh !—good morning.'

I never felt in such a rage in my life, and I nearly bawled out, ' You and your relatives may go to ' (any where you like) ' sir, for aught I care, and be hanged to you.' I was furious, I felt I had been so completely bamboozled and made such an utter fool of, but I *did* stifle my wrath, and I got out of the room and out of the house as quickly as I could.

All this occurred several years ago, and I have thought much about it ever since, and to this day I am in doubt as to what the old villain's exact intentions were; but I am inclined to think it was from beginning to end an artfully devised scheme to humiliate me—a plot carried out with deliberate malice and infinite cunning. On my soul, I believe he had never possessed the book at all, but I shall go to the sale of his library; and, only think too—he was nearly seventy years of age at the time !

What a malicious old cus' ! if ever I meet him in a spirit world, my spiritual finger and thumb shall tweak his spiritual pug-nose.

A DELICIOUS PICTURE.

‘ ’Twas in the road betwixt *Nismes* and *Lunel*, where there is the best *Muscatto* wine in all *France*. . . .The sun was set—they had done their work ; the nymphs had tied up their hair afresh—and the swains were preparing for a carousal.

‘ “ My mule made a dead point—“ ’Tis the fife and tambourin,” said I—“ I will never argue a point with one of your family as long as I live ; ” so leaping off his back, and kicking off one boot into this ditch, and t’other into that, “ I’ll take a dance,” said I—“ so stay you here.”

‘ A sun-burnt daughter of Labour rose up from the groupe to meet me, as I advanced towards them ; her hair, which was of a dark chestnut approaching rather to a black, was tied up in a knot, all but a single tress.

‘ “ We want a cavalier,” said she, holding out both her hands, as if to offer them—“ And a cavalier you shall have ; ” said I, taking hold of both of them. . . . “ We could not have done without you,” said she, letting go one hand, with self-taught politeness, leading me up with the other.

‘ A lame youth, whom *Apollo* had recompensed with a pipe, and to which he had added a tambourin of his own accord, ran sweetly over the prelude, as he sat upon the bank—“ Tie me up this tress, instantly,” said *Nanette*, putting a piece of string into my hand.—It taught me to forget I was a stranger—The whole knot fell down.—We had been seven years acquainted ! The youth struck the note upon the tambourin—his pipe followed, and off we bounded.

‘ The sister of the youth—who had stolen her voice from heaven—sang alternately with her brother. ’Twas a *Gascoigne* roundelay.

‘“ *Viva la joia ! fidon la tristessa !* ” the nymphs join’d in unison, and their swains an octave below them.

‘ *Viva la joia !* was in Nanette’s lips, *viva la joia !* was in her eyes. A transient spark of amity shot across the space betwixt us—she looked amiable ! Why could I not live, and end my days thus ? “ Just Disposer of our joys and sorrows,” cried I, “ why could not a man sit down in the lap of content here—and dance, and sing, and say his prayers, and go to Heaven with this nut-brown maid ? ’

‘ Capriciously did she bend her head on one side, and dance up insidious—

‘“ Then ’tis time to dance off,” quoth I—’

Laurence Sterne.

—•◇•—

A FABLE.

‘ A little boy had bought a Top,
The best in all the toyman’s shop ;
He made a whip with good eel’s-skin :
He lash’d the Top, and made it spin ;
All the children within call,

And the servants, one and all,
Stood round to see it and admire.
At last the Top began to tire,
He cried out, "Pray don't whip me, Master,
You whip too hard,—I can't spin faster,
I can spin quite as well without it."
The little Boy replied, " I doubt it ;
I only whip you for your good,
You were a foolish lump of wood,
By dint of whipping you were raised
To see yourself admired and praised,
And if I left you, you'd remain
A foolish lump of wood again." '

H. Frere (1769-1846).

The moral is so evident that it is omitted.

—◦◦—

QUAKERS AND BLUE-COAT BOYS.

The Rev. Sydney Smith wrote thus to Lady Morley :—

'Did you say a Quaker Baby? Impossible ! there is no such thing, there never was : they are always born broad-brimmed, and in full quake . . . Well, all I can say is, I never saw one, and what is still more remarkable I never met with any one who had. Have you heard the report that they are fed on drab, coloured pap? I have a theory about them and the Blue-Coat Boys.

'At a very early age young Quakers disappear,—at a very early age the Blue-Coat Boys are seen,—at the age of 17 or 18 young Quakers are again seen,—at the same age the Blue-Coat Boys disappear. Who has ever heard of a blue coat *man*! The thing is utterly unknown in Natural History. Upon what other evidence does the migration of the grub into the aurelia rest? Dissection would throw great light upon this question: and if our friend —— would receive two boys into his house about the time of their changing their coats, great service would be rendered to science.'

This was Lady Morley's reply: 'I should have said your theory and arguments were perfectly convincing, but I have come across a person who gives me information which puts us all at sea again. That the Blue-Coat Boy should be the larva of the Quaker in Great Britain is possible, and even probable. The Blue-Coat is an indigenous animal, not so the Quaker; and now be so good as to give your whole mind to the facts I have to communicate. Sir R. K. Porter has travelled over the whole habitable globe; he has lived for years in Philadelphia (the natural nest of the Quakers) and yet *he* has never seen a Quaker baby, and what is new, and most striking, never did he see a Quaker lady in a situation, which gave hope that a Quaker baby might be seen hereafter. This is a stunning fact, and involves the question in such impenetrable mystery as will, I fear, defy even your sagacity, acuteness, and industry to elucidate it, but let us not despair,' &c., &c.

This gracious fooling was carried on for some time longer. I believe the Rev. Sydney Smith ended by suggesting that an order should be obtained, through the Secretary of State, for the dissection of a Blue-Coat Boy, as he felt confident that, in doing so, the rudimentary Quaker would be discovered.

———◦✦◦———

THE MORALS OF THE NINETEENTH CENTURY.

It requires a certain capacity to be really good, the goodness of a great many people seems to be a mere incapacity for evil. Perhaps the superior morality of the present day is only an inferior criminality.

I heard Mr. Thomas Carlyle say something very like the above.

I know a good sort of man who began by 'going in for' being *spirituel* and wicked, and, failing in that, he is now a shining light in a company of respectable, but, as he would then have thought, *hum-drum* luminaries.

———◦✦◦———

MARRIAGE WITH A DECEASED WIFE'S SISTER.

It is asserted that if the advocates for marriage with a deceased wife's sister ever got the upper hand, they would become so tyrannical that they would make it obligatory on you to marry your deceased wife's sister. .

FINE-ART COLLECTORS.

Your fastidious fine-art collector is often an unhappy wretch. There is no end of mortification in store for him, and he has mainly himself to thank. It is his curse that from having been too credulous he ends by becoming over-sceptical, and believes everything that tells against himself and his collection.

You give your wife a *Rose du Barry* cup and saucer, which she mightily esteems, and of which you feel she has indeed just reason to be proud. It is exhibited with a good deal of pardonable vanity among your circle of acquaintance. A connoisseur spies it, whips it out of her little cabinet, examines it, praises it, smoothes its surface with his callous thumb, turns it round and round, turns it up, again admires it, and finally points out that, although the paste is all right, the decoration is dubious. You turn for comfort to another, an expert. He insists that the painting is entirely genuine, that your amateur is notoriously ignorant, and does not know 'a hawk from a handsaw'; but that, perhaps as regards the gilding, the less that is said about *that* the better, and then, horrid idea! he has a suspicion—only a suspicion, mind—that the saucer did not originally belong to the cup, and you are left in a pleasing state of doubt as to whether you should reveal your misgivings to your poor little wife.

The same with your favourite intaglio—a jacinth ; you purchased it as an antique, you paid a fabulous price for it, and yet you were given to understand by the vendor that he was doing you a great favour in letting you have it at all. You show it to a very experienced amateur, who has published a thick book upon the subject, he at once pronounces that it certainly is an antique, and he warmly congratulates you on having secured it ; but, says he, after a pause, ' My dear fellow, what a pity it has been repolished ' (and therefore spoilt !) and ' dear me,' as if he were making an agreeable and interesting discovery, 'perhaps a little worked upon, and at a comparatively recent date too, but what a charming specimen !' Another assures you it is of the *renaissance,* a *capo d'opera,* that *that* particular subject is *never* found on an antique gem ; while a third insists that it is altogether modern, that he has seen the original (a splendid sard) in a continental museum, in some out-of-the-way corner of the earth, say the museum at Cortona. It is of no use your assuring them that your poor little ring has been pronounced genuine at the British Museum ; all the *conoscenti,* outside the doors of that building, agree (and this is the only point on which they *do* agree) in declaring that the Museum is utterly and deplorably ignorant about gems.

Then your superb pen-drawing—a magnificent landscape by Titian ; it appears that, after all, it is *not* by Titian ; you are a lucky fellow, however, for there is no doubt it is, or rather *was*, a most important specimen of Dominico Campagnola, at least as far as it can be seen ; for, as another says, it has been a good deal rubbed, and restored, and gone over, so that it is difficult, at first, to say whom it is by. A third does not believe it is even of the *scuola* of Campagnola, he has, come upon exactly the same composition in the Albertina, a sumptuous silver-point drawing, and he suggests that your drawing is by an adroit copyist of the eighteenth century, whose name is not even known, but whose works, your informant says, are to be found in every collection on the Continent, and are, in fact, as plentiful as blackberries.

It is much the same with your poor old books. You gave 10*l*. for, say, the ' Salisbury' edition of the ' Vicar of Wakefield,' and had it bound in morocco, by Bedford ; and your friend, and rival collector, tells you he has just secured the same book IN THE ORIGINAL BLUE COB'S-PAPER COVERS, out of a country book-seller's catalogue for eighteen-pence ! ' and altogether a more interesting copy, for that matter,' for, it would appear, his has certain ' cancelled leaves,' which yours does not possess. Indeed, you may esteem yourself lucky if, after all, you do not find out that one of your title-pages is in ' such admirable facsimile as *almost*

' to defy detection.'   Heigh ho! Hark how the poet '
moralizes on what the miserable collector has to look
forward to :—

> ' Then, Richard, then should we sit down,
> Far from the tumult of this town;
> I fond of my well-chosen seat,
> My pictures, medals, books complete.
> Or, should we mix our friendly talk,
> O'er-shaded in that favourite walk
> Which thy own hand had whilom planted,
> Both pleased with all we thought we wanted :
> Yet then, even then, one cross reflection
> Would spoil thy grove, and my collection :
> Thy son (and his, ere that) may die,
> And time some uncouth heir supply;
> Who shall for nothing else be known
> But spoiling all that thou hast done.
> Who set the twigs shall he remember
> That is in haste to sell the timber?
> And what shall of thy goods remain—
> Except the box that threw the main?
>   Nay, may not time and death remove
> The dear relations whom I love?
> And my coz Tom, or his coz Mary
> (Who hold the plough, or skim the dairy),
> My favourite books and pictures sell,
> To Smart, or Doily by the ell?

Those who could never read their grammar,
When my dear Volumes touch the hammer,
May think books best as richest bound ;
My copper medals by the pound
May be with learnèd justice weigh'd ;
To turn the balance, Otho's head
May be thrown in : and, for the metal,
The coin may mend a tinker's kettle,'
&c., &c.

'Alma,' Matthew Prior (1664–1721).

'Little children, keep yourselves from idols.'

MUSIC AND PAINTING.

Some one remarked of the portrait of the Rev.
Holwell Carr (who, tradition declares, was a carping
and sceptical art-critic) that it looked as if in the act
of saying 'Yes, but the original is in the Borghese
Gallery.' I should rather like to see a collection of
the portraits of the art-critics of the present day.

Art-criticism in England is in a very unsatisfactory
condition. There is very little which is really sound,
and that is the criticism which is least heard of. Then
all the art-critics are at odds, and about everything,
and this will continue to be the case as long as 'the
many-headed beast' is so indifferent, so presumptuous,
and so ignorant. We judge of music by the eye and

painting by the ear. I respect that honest fellow who remarked that Jenny Lind would have been an entirely delightful person—but for her singing.

———◆◇◆———

FINE-ART COLLECTORS.

A collector of pictures, going abroad, innocently asked where genuine works by the Old Masters were to be picked up. ' Go to Bologna,' said his friend, confidently. ' Go to Bologna—there are no bad pictures in Bologna now, for Lord Blank has just bought them all.'

———◆◇◆———

RIDDLE.

Why are the birds unhappy in their nests in the early morning?

Because their poor little bills are all over due (dew).

———◆◇◆———

THEODORE HOOK.

In Theodore Hook the passion for mischief was inveterate and ineradicable. There is a registering barometer in the hall of the Athenæum Club, close to the door, placed there for the convenience and guidance of members; and Hook, even after middle life, had a difficulty in passing this instrument without disarranging it, and thus rendering it an entirely false guide to those who would consult it. He was an impudent fellow, too, for, in his younger days, in the street, he would walk up to any rather pompous, self-satisfied looking gentleman, and, taking off his hat, say, with a respectful and inquiring air, 'I beg your pardon, sir, but are you anybody in particular?' An acquaintance of Douglas Jerrold's once came up to him and said, in an aggrieved tone, 'What is this, Jerrold? I hear you have been saying my nose is like the ace of clubs.' 'No, I didn't,' said Jerrold, 'but, now that I look at your nose, I see it is very like.' Theodore Hook would have been quite capable of saying this. He was once asked what kind of sport leap-frog was; and to describe it, he rather irreverently made use of the tuneful names of Stern-hold and Hop-kins.

LOVE IN THE VALLEY.

'Under yonder beech-tree, standing on the green
    sward,
Couched with her arms behind her little head,
Her knees folded up, and her tresses on her bosom,
    Lies my young love, sleeping in the shade.
Had I the heart to slide one arm beneath her!
    Press her dreaming lips as her waist I folded slow,
Waking on the instant, she could not but embrace me—
    Ah, would she hold me, and never let me go?

' Shy as the squirrel, and wayward as the swallow,
    Swift as the swallow when athwart the western
      flood,
Circleting the surface, he meets his mirror'd winglets,
    Is that dear one in her maiden bud.
Shy as the squirrel whose nest is in the pine-tops ;
    Gentle, ah, that she was jealous as the dove !
Full of all the wildness of the woodland creatures,
    Happy in herself is the maiden that I love.!

' What can have taught her distrust of all I tell her ?
    Can she truly doubt me when looking on my brows?
Nature never teaches distrust of tender love-tales,
    What can have taught her distrust of all my vows ?
No, she does not doubt me ! on a dewy eve-tide
    Whispering together beneath the listening moon,
I pray'd till her cheek flush'd, implored till she
    faltered,
    Flutter'd to my bosom—ah, to fly away so soon !

' When her mother tends her before the laughing mirror,
    Tying up her laces, looping up her hair,
Often she thinks—"Were this wild thing wedded,
    I should have more love—and much less care."
When her mother tends her before the bashful mirror,
    Loosening her laces, combing down her curls,
Often she thinks—" Were this wild thing wedded;
    I should lose but one for so many boys and girls."

'Clambering roses peep into her chamber,
  Jasmine and woodbine breathe sweet, sweet,
White-neck'd swallows twittering of summer,
  Fill her with balm, and nested peace from head to
    feet.
Ah, will the rose-bough see her lying lonely,
  When the petals fall, and fierce bloom is on the
    leaves?
Will the autumn garners see her still ungather'd,
  When the fickle swallows forsake the weeping eaves?

'When at dawn she wakens, and her fair face gazes
  Out on the weather, thro' the window panes,
Beauteous she looks! like a white water-lily,
  Bursting out of bud on the rippled river plains.
When from bed she rises, clothed from neck to ankle
  In her long night-gown, sweet as boughs of May,
Beauteous she looks, like a tall garden-lily,
  Pure from the night, and perfect for the day!

'Happy, happy time when the grey star twinkles
  Over the fields, all fresh with blooming dew;
When the cold-cheeked dawn grows ruddy up the
    twilight,
  And the gold sun wakes, and weds her in the blue.
Then when my darling tempts the early breezes,
  She the only star that dies not with the dark!
Powerless to speak all the ardour of my passion
  I catch her little hand as we listen to the lark.

'Shall the birds in vain then, Valentine, their sweet-
    hearts,
  Season after season, tell a fruitless tale?
Will not the virgin listen to their voices,
  Take the honey'd meaning, wear the bridal veil?
Fears she frosts of winter, fears she the bare branches,
  Waits she the garland of spring for her dower?
Is she a nightingale that will not be nested
  Till the April woodland has built her bridal bower?

'Then come, merry April, with all thy birds and
    beauties!
  With thy crescent brows, and thy flowery, showery
    glee;
With thy budding leafage, and fresh green pastures;
  And may thy lustrous crescent grow a honeymoon
    for me!
Come, merry month of the cuckoo and the violet!
  Come, weeping loveliness, in all thy blue delight!
Lo! the nest is ready, let me not languish longer,
  Bring her to my arms on the first May night.'

George Meredith.

.*. We can picture to ourselves the boy Poet
of these charming lines, like Keats, hardly out of his
teens.

JOHN WESLEY,

(1703-1791).

I have a very long and curious autograph letter addressed by John Wesley to his wife, 'Dear Molly,' and dated Coleford, Oct 23, 1759.

It is a curious and most pitiable complaint of her conduct. He remonstrates with her for appropriating his money, and stealing his papers, for lying, and for treating his servants like dogs. In conclusion he says, 'These are the advices which I now give you, in the fear of God, and in tender love to your soul. Nor can I give you a stronger proof that I am your affectionate husband.'

I do not know whether Mrs. Wesley laid this letter to heart, but she had evidently read it very carefully, for she has made autograph notes upon it in three or four places ; for instance, where her husband says her conduct *may drive him further off*, she has written the word ' *imposable*.'

A GOOD REASON.

A large landed proprietor had been murdered in Ireland, and a car-driver was telling his fare how universally he had been execrated on his estate, when the gentleman naturally enough remarked, ' Then the wonder is that he was not put to death long ago.' ' Och, your Honour,' said Paddy, 'that's how it is, you know—what's everybody's business is nobody's business.'

THE CLIMATE OF IRELAND.

Irishman.—'Ireland's the finist climate in the world.'

Stranger.—'Yes, I believe you have very little frost or snow.'

Irishman.—'Oh, plinty, sir, plinty of frost and snow, but frost and snow is not cold in Ireland.'

(Probably he meant to say *not disagreeable.*)

REAL HUMILITY.

The Vicar met a poor parish girl, who had been in service, and had got married the week before. 'Well, Sally,' said he, 'and how do you like matrimony?' She replied, and with exquisite humility, 'I like it very much, sir' (curtsey). 'It's beautiful sir' (curtsey). 'It's too good for a poor girl like me.'

AN INTRACTABLE BRIDEGROOM AND ONE MORE TRACTABLE.

A couple presenting themselves to be married, the clergyman objected that the bridegroom was tipsy, and therefore, very properly, refused to perform the cere-mony. A few days afterwards the same thing occurred with the same couple; whereupon the clergyman gravely expostulated with the bride, and said that they must not present themselves again with the bridegroom in that condition. 'But, sir,'—she naïvely exclaimed—'he won't come when he's sober.'

This could hardly be the bridegroom who when the clergyman said 'Wilt thou have this woman to be thy wedded wife,' unhesitatingly replied—'In course I will, sir, why I come here a-purpose.'

THE LADY AND THE CABMAN.

Lady C——, a very agreeable and amiable woman, took a cab to the house of a friend; on alighting she observed that cabby was tipsy. After she had taken the precaution of ringing the bell, she gave him his fare, and said, with severity and reproachfully, 'I have hired many cabs, and this is the first time I have been driven by a tipsy cabman.' This was cabby's emphatic and incisive rejoinder—'I was never soberer in my life; it's *you* that have been a-drinkin'—*you knows you have.* You ought to be ashamed o' yourself.'

Lady C—— was not sorry that at that moment the front door opened.

A LOVER'S MESSAGE.

'Ye little nymphs that hourly wait
To bring from Cælia's eyes my fate,
Tell her my pain in softest sighs,
And gently whisper Strephon dies.
But if this won't her pity move,
And the coy nymph disdains to love,
Tell her, again, 'tis all a lie,
And haughty Strephon scorns to die.'

Earl of Kellie.

SPORT.

'He had catched a great cold had he had none other clothes to wear than the skin of a bear not yet killed.'

The other day I tumbled on this passage in Fuller, and here, among the lonely hills, it has set me athinking on all the curious vicissitudes of sport, whether it be the pursuit of fishes, or of birds, or of four-footed creatures—including bears.

Let us suppose, now, that I go a-fishing. I am encouraged to do so by those who are reputed to be weather-wise, but who prove to be quite otherwise. My pony takes me in less than half-an-hour to the loch. The wind is in the south. There is enough of it. I whip the water, I go on whipping it; but, some-

how, I cannot get a rise out of it. The sky is fairly
covered. The water is of the right colour, in fact
everything seems as favourable for the sport as possible, but, at last the old Gael (not the old Gael who
plies the sculls, but the other, the more ancient Gael,
who superintends the sport) suggests, 'Maybe there's
joost a wee bit thunner in the air.' I think he says
this, but his vocabulary is so scant, and his accent so
individual that I can't be certain. Yesterday he had
assured me that the sun was too bright. The day
before that there was much too little 'wund,' and the
day before that, that I had not the proper description
of fly—I happened to have a '*hare's lug*,' when, of
course, I ought to have had a '*coachman*.' He now
tells me that if I had *only* brought a 'phantom'
minnow with me, I might have done something, but
that, as it is, he fears it is a bad look-out : and then
he relates a tantalising anecdote of a certain General
Foster who had fished the loch some years before, on
just such another day as this, and in just this part of
the loch, too, and how he had caught twelve-score
trout before luncheon, and not one of them less than
a pound and a half. All this time I have been whipping away without any result whatever, and I begin to
despair, and this being the case I make up my mind
that *my* twelve-score fish shall be secured *after* luncheon, so I fall to. I hate sandwiches without mustard
—but, hillo !—here's a little pat of that excellent butter

—but where's the knife? They've forgotten the knife! So I am obliged to spread my butter with the cork-screw. After luncheon I again whip, whip, whip the water, but without avail, so for exercise, and also because I have nothing better to do, before returning home, I row the two old gentlemen about the loch, and so ends my long day's fishing.

Then as regards the grouse, or the partridge, or the pheasant, or the capercailzie, or the tom-tit, for it is all one which it is, there are no end of disappointments and humiliations in store for those who pursue them. Let me tell you two little anecdotes on the subject, and they are foolish enough, so I beg that I may not be identified with the hero of either of them.

A friend of mine had a game-keeper who was an original, and often expressed himself very incisively. One day he was in the cover with a neighbour who invariably missed everything he aimed at. A pheasant got up, the neighbour blazed away, some feathers flew, and he exclaimed in a voice of natural exultation, 'I hit him that time, Cox, and no mistake.' The man's reply was characteristic: 'Ah, sir, they *will* fly into it, sometimes.'

The other story was of a foreigner, rabbit-shooting in the shires, and continually missing his quarry—who complained that the rabbits were so very short in England! Sportsmen have their troubles, and so

have the ornithologists, and so have the poor birds
themselves, for that matter. Hearken to the poet
laureate of 1670 :

> ' As callow birds
> Whose mother's killed in seeking of the prey,
> Cry in their nest, and think her long away,
> And at each leaf that stirs, each blast of wind,
> Gape for the food which they must never find.'

All that has been previously said, however, is as
nothing to the stalking of deer. I was on the hill
yesterday, the weather was misty as we left the lodge,
it grew worse as we climbed Ben Pityoulish, and it
ended in our having to sit two full hours in the drizzle,
communing with our own hearts ; during the whole of
which time we were subjects of considerable interest to
the flies ; at last the mist arose, then we arose also,
and got out our glasses and spied for two hours
more.

It would be weariful for me to tell you of all the
vicissitudes connected with trying for a stag, indeed
you would lose your patience if I attempted it, but just
let us suppose you are on the stalking-ground, and that
you have sighted your quarry. The herd consists, say,
of ten stags, some are rather small, some are in velvet,
and there is a switch head, but one of them is a magnificent fellow, a royal, weighing, as near as your
stalker can judge, full eighteen stone, and quite clean.

They are 'a wee wust' of you on the sky line, and there are only a few knobbies, composed of scars and peat hags, between you and them. You are stiffish, for you have been crouching for some hours in a slack behind a humpie, with your feet in a shallow pool of water, and your person devoured by mosquitoes, but you are now to be rewarded for your masterly inactivity; yes, the hour for action is at hand—that is to say, if the wind does not change ; if it shifts, or as Donald Bean, the stalker, would put it, 'if the wund swirls maybe they'll get a blink o't.' That means if the herd gets your wind you are done for. Luckily there is a shallowish burn, and you commence working your way along it, through the ripple, on your hands and knees, for about a quarter of an hour—your stalker is before you, and your second on the stalk is behind you. Your stalker, every now and again, straightens himself, and stops to spy. Your royal is still where he was, just at the edge of a clearing, but three of the herd have moved on, feeding : however, your royal is still there, and improves on nearer acquaintance—he is over eighteen stone, *per Bacco*, there is no doubt about it, and he has a *groff* black head with white points ! Will the wind shift ? If it does shift you are a *gone coon.* Just at this moment you hear the *croak croak* of a pair of ravens over your head, and you esteem it a good omen.

Well, the affair is becoming exciting. Your stalker

is getting dreadfully keen, I may say as keen as mustard. He whispers that you are now within some eighty yards of the herd. Your royal is feeding, but he is feeding *from* you. You can't let fly for fear of disturbing his haunches, but *you* can now count his points. Your stalker slips your rifle out of its case, and reaches it to you ; you cock it—when—all of a sudden—not twenty yards in front of you—just above a big bluestone, you catch the twinkle of a pair of ears—exasperating sight ! *it is a hind !*—a hind that none of you had observed ! She is between you and your quarry, and you know she will give the alarm. She *does* give the alarm, for off springs the royal (alas now no longer *yours*), end on, and he and the rest of the herd disappear behind the shoulder of the knobbie in front of you, and you sit down on a stone in collapse.

So much for your *luck*. Yes ! that's it—the luck is against you ; if it had not been a hind, it would have been a covey of grouse, or a roe, or a black-cock, and either would have been fatal—yes, your stag would have been equally scared, and as inevitably lost— hang you luck !

The day thus described may be considered a fairly successful one. For you *did* get your stalk, and, *this time*, your rifle did *not* miss fire, and your foot did *not* slip on a loose stone at the instant of pulling the trigger, or a thousand other contingencies equally condemnable. Yes, it was not so bad, for are you not out day after

day from 8 A.M. to 8 P.M., passing the majority of those
hours drenched to the skin, and devoured by the flies,
as you sweep the distant corries with your glass, or
take a wistful spy at the sanctuary?

When after such an expedition you get back to the
lodge, and are in cool blood, it might perchance occur
to you that after all you have never been much nearer
to your stag than you were ere you set out in the
morning—that your wife has been almost as near while
she sat before her peat fire, with her embroidery in her
lap, or her nose in a book.

And what book shall we give her? Shall it be
some gentle protest against what is, or rather ought
to be, going forward on the hill yonder? Is it the
music of one whose delight it was, in summer shade,
to pipe a simple song for thinking hearts? We
hearken to the old wizard, and lo, we are at once
on enchanted ground. He tells us of a forlorn
place, where, many and many a year before, a pitiless
deed had been done, and he says that to judge
from its aspect it would seem as if the spring-time
came not there, and nature there seemed willing to
decay. How the lovely verses linger in the memory!
Then he approaches that Being who maintains a deep
and reverential care for the unoffending creatures whom
He loves. And then, with solemn sweetness, he adjures
us never to blend our pleasure or our pride with sorrow

of the meanest thing that feels.   Fair lady, we might
give you a worse book than that !

As I sit here, beneath a fair sky, and listen to the
sound of running waters; the everlasting hills, a shining
circle around me, and an abounding ocean of deep
purple heather about me, the keen air gives a sting
to my blood, and sends it more buoyantly through my
veins, and my regenerate spirit recoils from all this
cockney babble in mockery of a robust emprise, the
vicissitudes and triumphs of which have interested me
so long, and given me such genuine delight.

But may not there be some luckless yet sympathetic soul, some tearful jester, some toiler within
sound of St. Stephen's big bell, who (a stranger to
this noble strath and its enchanting surroundings)
may yet be able to extract amusement, I would fain
have said *solace*, from my poor little sketch ?   If so,
I thank him, but let him not come here to read it :
this is the last spot on God's earth that he should
choose.

Dear reader, if you are such a man, whoever or
whatever you may be, I wish you well ; and what better
could I desire for you than that you should toss this
volume into the kennel, and come and enjoy the
sports about which I have so gracelessly jested ?

A DAY'S SPORT.

I believe this was Thomas Hood's account of his friend's day's shooting : 'What he hit is history, and what he missed is mystery'—(*his story and my story*).

A STRANGE NOISE.

Archdeacon M. was calling on one of his parishioners, who suffered grievously from a noise in his head. In reply to his sympathetic inquiries, the sufferer's wife told him that the noise was occasionally 'so bad,' that sometimes she 'thought it must be the people in the next public house !'

A CURIOUS PANACEA.

A woman who was not a physiologist, and whose husband had some internal malady, said to a friend of mine, 'You see, madam, I gives him a deal of bread and milk. It flies to the part, you know, and acts as a poultice.'

A BAPTISMAL DIFFICULTY.

A French priest was baptising an infant ; he had a new *livre d'office* and he could not find the service, and said, with irritability, 'C'est un enfant très difficile à baptiser.'

———◇———

HEIRS.

A clergyman catechising a class in a village school, and speaking of their being heirs to the kingdom of heaven, asked a small boy, ' What is an heir ?' *Small boy* : ' A little beastie, like a rabbut.'

———◇———

PHOTOGRAPHING DOWN WEST.

An American newspaper states that a Nevada photographer takes very decided measures for turning out a good portrait. The sitter being in his place, the artist produces a navy revolver, cocks it, and levels it at the sitter's head, and says, ' Now, just you sit perfectly still, and don't move a hair ; put on a calm pleasant expression of countenance, and look right into the muzzle of this revolver, or I'll blow the top of your head off. My reputation as an artist is at stake, and I don't want no nonsense about this picture.'

———◇———

SETTLERS.

An Englishman met a party of American settlers journeying westward, and got into conversation with

their leader, a practical man.   He said, 'We only take
useful people with us.   This,' pointing to a man, 'is our
joiner ;' of another, 'this is our blacksmith ;' of a third,
'this is our baker,' and so on. 'But,' said the Englishman,
'That very old fellow, surely he can't be of much use
to you.' 'Oh yes,' says the man, 'he is.   That's grandfather ; we shall open our new cemetery with him.'

EPITAPH ON DENYS ROLLE, OF BICTON.

'His earthly part within this tomb doth rest,
Who kept a court of honour in his breast ;
Birthe, Beauty, witt, and wisedome sate as Peeres,
Till Death mistook his virtues for his yeares,
Or else Heaven envied Earth so rich a treasure,
Wherein too fine the ware, too scant the measure.
His mournful wife, her love to show in part,
This tombe built here a better in her heart.
Sweet Babe, his hopeful Heyre (Heaven grant this
        boon),
Live but so well ; but, oh, dye not so soon.'

Thomas Fuller (1608-1661).

INNATE IDEAS.

'Our ideas, like the children of our youth, often die
before us, and our minds represent to us those tombs

to which we are fast approaching—where, though the brass and marble may remain, the inscriptions are effaced by time and the imagery moulders away.'

John Locke (1632–1704).

THE MILLENNIUM IN INVERNESS.

Miss C——, an old spinster lady of Inverness, tired of hearing some of her friends continually talking of the Millennium, and thinking, perhaps, they talked nonsense about it, indignantly broke forth one day in these words : ' What for are they always talkin' aboot the Millennium? I mind when there *was* a Millennium in Inverness ; if ye met a friend in the street, it was always, " When are ye comin' to my hoos ?—ye maun fust cum to my hoos "—and balls and pairties, and the gentlemen comin' in sae merry after denner—that *was* a Millennium indeed ! '

AN AFFAIR OF THE HEART.

A gentleman was seated in the stage coach opposite to a young lady who looked delicate, and appeared suffering. When the coach stopped, and the young lady alighted, the gentleman took the opportunity of asking her female attendant if she was consumptive. ' No, sir,' replied her nurse, 'it is her heart that is

affected.' 'How very sad ! Is it aneurism?' 'Oh,
no, sir,' said the woman, 'it is a young Lieutenant in
the Royal Navy.'

———◦◦———

SHORT PEOPLE.

'Tall men are like tall houses, often poorly furnished
in the top story.'

My dear father was a little man, and a rigid
moralist. One day, when I was quite a small child,
I was walking with him in London, he leading me by
the hand, and we met a Sir Joseph Greensides, a fat-
headed old Christian, and a very big man. Sir Joseph
stopped, and spoke a few words to my father, and I
noticed that my father gazed up at him with a keen
expression of distaste. When they parted, my father
looked down at me with a sardonic smile, and said (as
if he were taking me into his confidence) : 'That's a
nice little infant, eh !' After a minute, he added, and
with energy, 'He is a jobber,' and then said no more.

I could not have been above seven years old when
this happened, yet I have never forgotten it. I was
afraid of my father, but somehow, even then, it
occurred to me that he would not have felt quite so
strongly if the old boy had not been quite so big. •

Sir Joseph has long gone over to the majority ; he
had a bald head, and large carroty whiskers, which
made some people call him Sir Joseph *Red*sides, a

M

circumstance hardly worth recording. I ought to add that my excellent father was fully justified in both his remarks.

----•◦•----

BARONETS.

A man had a title conferred upon him. A cynical friend congratulated him on the honour. 'A knighthood, eh?' 'No,' says he, with dignity, 'a baronetcy.' 'I'm sorry for you,' said his friend. 'Why so?' replied the baronet. 'Oh, because if you had been made a knight, you know, at any rate the infamy would have died with you.'

Apropos of baronets, some people say they know when there is a 'comely careful mousing cat' in the room. I know a man, a queer creature, who has made up his mind that he hates baronets, and in a similar way he pretends he is instantly aware of the presence of one when he enters a room.

----•◦•----

LOVE'S LAST MESSAGE.

'Merry, merry little stream,
　　Tell me, hast thou seen my dear?
I left him with an azure dream,
　　Calmly sleeping on his bier—
　　　　But he has fled!

" I passed him in his churchyard bed,
A yew is sighing o'er his head,
And grass-roots mingle with his hair."
    ' What doth he there?
O cruel, can he lie alone?
 Or in the arms of one more dear?
Or hides he in the bower of stone,
 To cause, and kiss away my fear?

' " He doth not speak, he doth not moan—
Blind, motionless he lies alone :.
But ere the grave-snake flesh'd his sting,
This one warm tear he bade me bring
   And lay it at thy feet
   Among the daisies sweet."

' Moonlight whisperer, summer air,
 Songster of the groves above,
Tell the maiden-rose I wear
 Whether thou hast seen my love.
" This night in heaven I saw him lie,
   Discontented with his bliss ;
   And on my lips he left this kiss,
For thee to taste and then to die." '

     Thomas Lovell Beddoes (1802-1849).

STRONG LANGUAGE.

Oaths are not altogether to be commended, but, at the same time, it has been remarked that nobody can swear with all his heart and soul unless he has a real belief in a special Providence and a future state.

I was once in a well-filled omnibus, and something occurred which excited the wrath of an elderly gentleman who sat by the door. He took to swearing at the conductor, and at such a rate that the passengers began to think he would never leave off; he did, however, at last, and after glaring fiercely about him, he bounced out of the vehicle—stem last.

There was a meek-looking old lady seated near me, and when he was gone she remarked to me in a low voice, ' *I think, sir, that gentleman must have been an Admiral.*' I was struck with the observation, and I now recognise its force. There is no doubt that *old Admirals* are, as a body, more or less devout, and it is equally true they are addicted to—what shall I call it?—to forcible language.

For instance, there was my father's friend, Admiral Sir R—— K——. When I was a child he sometimes patted my head, and I stood in great awe of him. He was a most distinguished officer, and the only polished gentleman I can call to mind who swore habitually and lustily in the society of ladies, and that, too, in the most high-bred manner. Sir R——, a staunch champion for

church and king, was not an old Admiral of many words,
' he did na $ay muckle, but, oh, he damned bonny ! '

Then I have been told that Sir Herbert Taylor
once found himself in the presence of that gallant old
Admiral, as well as really good man, his Royal master,
when he happened to be admonishing his tailor,
who had not carried out his sartorial engagements in
a satisfactory manner. ' *Bless* you to *Heaven*, sir,'
shouted his Majesty, and *bless* your wife, sir, and your
blest children, and all your *blest* family,' and then,
having provided for all the tailor's relations, His
Majesty, as the Highlander would have described it,
"juist stude in ta middle of ta room, and swoor at
lairge," during which exercise Sir Herbert discreetly
put his helm hard a-port, and withdrew. I am sure
the old lady in the omnibus was right.

Apropos of this style of conversation, it has never
been confined to high life. Not long ago I was walking in York Street, Westminster, which used to be the
favourite rendezvous of some of the poorest and most
abject wretches in all London. I noticed a young
woman, with a baby in her arms, standing upon the
door-step of a public-house. She was bending over
her child, and I was struck with the look of rapture on
her homely countenance—that expression of motherly
love and joy, than which there is nothing more beautiful in nature, and which for the moment seemed to
glorify her. She was fondling and talking to it, and

there was little to object to in the sentiments she expressed, excepting that all her expletives were breaches
of the Third Commandment, and her few terms of
endearment were so coarse that you would not care
that they should be recorded here. It was her ordinary
language, she knew no other. We are taught that
mortals are answerable for all their idle words—it
is not for me to gauge that young person's responsi-
bilities.

In recent hill warfare with the Afreedees, who are
human beings not a whit more degraded than the
aborigines of Westminster, some of the native population zealously took our side. On one occasion an
officer on duty pointed out to a native sentry a certain
black fellow whom he had observed skulking, with
others round the fort, evidently with sinister intentions.
' I see him, sar,' said the sentry—'had two shots at him
a'ready, him dam hard to hit, he hardest man to hit
I know.' ' Oh, you know him, do you?' said the officer.
' Oh, yes, sar, I know de dam rascal. I been tryin' to
shoot him all de week.' ' Well, who is he? What's
his name?' ' Oh, de dam rascal—he my father.'

Something of the same kind may be said of an
elderly South Sea Islander, who was observed peering
over a pool in the rocks, and on being asked how he
lived, and what he did, he replied, with his very
limited command of English, ' Pokin' dam crabs, out
dam hole, with dam stick'—an unconscious satire

on the scope of English invention in the art of cursing.

Oaths are occasionally used in the very queerest fashion and on the most incongruous occasions. I have heard of a man anathematising the law of gravitation because he had tumbled down and hurt himself. Then Hogg, the Shepherd-Poet, was a touchy man, and after his quarrel with Scott (who never quarrelled with anybody) he wrote Scott a fierce letter, which began, *'Damned* Sir,' &c. ; and again, if you turn to that interesting reprint of the first edition of the ‚'Pilgrim's Progress' (Mr. Holford has the only, or almost the only, copy of the original known to exist), you will see that John Bunyan describes Christian's path to the valley of the Shadow of Death as being *'Damnably* muddy.'

A citizen of the United States of America, on being admonished for using strong language, thus excused himself : *' You* wouldn't say the Lord's Prayer if you'd trod upon the *business* end of a tin tack.'

---·◦·---

THE GRAVES OF THE COVENANTERS.

'There are few more interesting episodes in Modern Ecclesiastical History than that of the Scottish Covenanters. But the school in which that episode must be studied is Scotland itself. The caves, and moors, and moss-hags of the Western Lowlands ; the tales, which linger still, of the black charger of Claverhouse, of the strange encounters with the Evil One, of the cry of the plover and peewit round the encampments on the hill-side, are more instructive than many books. The rude gravestones which mark the spots where those were laid who bore testimony to "the covenanted work of reformation," and " Christ's kingly government of His house," bring before us in the most lively, because in the most condensed, authentic, original form, the excited feeling of the time, and the most peculiar traits of the religion of the Scottish people. Their independence, their fervour, their fierceness, may have belonged to the age. But hardly out of Scotland could be found their stubborn endurance, their thirst for vengeance, their investment of the narrowest questions of discipline and ceremony with the sacredness of universal principles. We almost fancy that we see the survivors of the dead spelling and scooping out their savage rhymes on the simple monuments—each catching from each the epithets, the texts, the names, almost Homeric in the simplicity and the sameness with which they are repeated on those lonely tomb-stones from shore to shore of the Scottish kingdom.'

Arthur P. Stanley, Dean of Westminster.

CONUNDRUM.

A. What do you do with your eyes?

B. I do not know.

A. Do not you dot them?

B. Oh yes, of course, I dot them.

A. But you ought not to dot them.

B. Why not?

A. Why, because they are *capital* eyes.

CHAOS AND THE CREATION.

Hans Sachs (who lived 1494-1576) describing Chaos, said it was so pitchy dark that even the cats ran against each other.

I do not know whether the exigencies of the drama require it, but there is a German play, in which, when the curtain rises, our first parent Adam is discovered crossing the stage—going to be created.

AN ENGLISH CLERGYMAN.

The following was a black Australian's description of an English clergyman : 'White fellow, belonging to Sunday, wear 'im shirt over trouser, get up in tree, and make long corrobory-bobbery all 'bout debil, debil.'

AN ENTHUSIAST IN GRAMMAR.

The good Abbé de Dangeau, when he received the tidings of the disasters of Ramillies and Blenheim, said, as he affectionately laid his hand on his old bureau, ‘Come what may, I have safe here three thousand verbs all correctly conjugated.’

TO HIS SONNE.

‘ Three things thear bee, that prosper all apace,
   And flourish while they are asunder farr;
But on a day, they meet all in a place,
   And when they meet they one another marre.

‘ And they be these ; the Wood, the Weed, the Wagge :
   The Wood is that that makes the gallowes tree !
The Weed is that which strings the hangman’s bagge ;
   The Wagge, my pretty knave, betokens thee.

‘ Now marke, dear boy, while these assemble not,
   Greene springes the tree, hemp growes, the Wagge
      is wild ;
But when they meet it makes the timber rot,
   It fretts the halter, and it choakes the child.
                     God bless the child ! ’

                     Sir Walter Raleigh (1552–1618).

HAYDN.

In setting the Ten Commandments to music, Haydn, the composer, with grim humour, stole a melody for the eighth.

———◦◦———

FORTITUDE AND PIETY.

'After the robbers' (who had plundered and stripped him) 'were gone, I sat for some time looking around me with amazement and terror. Whichever way I turned, nothing appeared but danger and difficulty. I saw myself in the midst of a vast wilderness, in the depth of the rainy season, naked and alone, surrounded by savage animals, and men still more savage. I was five hundred miles from the nearest European settlement. All these circumstances crowded at once upon my recollection, and I confess that my spirits began to fail me. I considered my fate as certain, and that I had no alternative but to lie down and perish. The influence of religion, however, aided and supported me. I reflected that no human prudence or foresight could possibly have averted my present sufferings. I was indeed a stranger in a strange land, yet I was still under the protecting eye of that Providence who has condescended to call Himself the stranger's friend.

'At this moment, painful as my reflections were,

the extraordinary beauty of a small moss in fructifica-
tion irresistibly caught my eye. I mention this to show
from what trifling circumstances the mind will sometimes derive consolation, for though the whole plant
was not larger than the top of one of my fingers, I
could not contemplate the delicate conformation of its
roots, leaves and capsula, without admiration. Can that
Being, thought I, who planted, watered, and brought to
perfection, in this remote part of the world, a thing
which appears of so small importance, look with
unconcern upon the situation and sufferings of
creatures formed after His own image? Surely not.
Reflections like these would not allow me to despair.
I started up, and, disregarding both hunger and fatigue,
travelled forwards, assured that relief was at hand.'

Mungo Park (1771–1805).

And he was not disappointed, for shortly afterwards
he reached a village where he found shelter and succour.

HUMAN LIFE.

. . . . 'This earthy load
Of Death called life, which us from Life doth sever.'

Speaking of Philistinism, Mr. Matthew Arnold
says : 'We have not the expression in English ; perhaps we have not the word because we have so much of
the thing. At Soli, I imagine, they did not talk of sole-
cisms, and here, at the very head-quarters of Goliath,

nobody talks of Philistinism. It means a strong,
'dogged, unenlightened opponent of the chosen people,
of the children of light—the would-be remodellers
of the old traditional European order, the invokers
of reason against custom, the representatives of the
modern Spirit in every sphere where it is applic-
able. Regarding themselves, with the robust self-
confidence natural to reformers, as a chosen people,
as children of the light, they regarded the Philistines,
as humdrum people, slaves to routine, enemies to
light, stupid and oppressive; but, at the same time,
very strong. . . The born lover of ideas, the born
hater of commonplaces, must feel, in this country,
that the sky over his head is of brass or iron.'

It has often struck us that Philistines are a
nuisance, but our dissatisfaction and discouragement
goes deeper than Philistinism. We complain that we
have been pitched-forked on a planet for which
morally and physically we are altogether unsuited,
where our existence is a long drawn-out malady, for
which there is no certain cure but churchyard mould.
Yes, you have only to walk into the street, and you
will observe that this consuming care and incurable
melancholy is written on every face you meet. We do
what we can, we cling to our illusions, we try to forget
our disappointments and to dissemble our miseries,
and what is the comfort held out to us? We are assured that it is quite an illusion, that we are not miser-

able, we are happy, and ought to be so, that we have
been placed on this earth for a wise purpose, by a
Power which takes a personal interest in our well-
being, that whatever misery and crime there are, are
mysteries, and mysteries we cannot fathom, but that all
is working for our ultimate welfare; that the free will
accorded to us 'is a kind of natural sovereignty over
ourselves, to govern ourselves ;' in fine, that the worth
of our life is to be measured by its activity in the path
of duty; that the measure of its worth is not the joy
or misery found in the world, but in the satisfaction
that follows free and right activity.   All this sounds
comforting, and, indeed, we would fain believe it; and
sometimes, when the wind is not in the east, we *do*
believe it :

> 'Ah, yes, when all is thought and said,
> The heart still overrules the head ;
> Still what we hope we must believe,
> And what is given us receive.
>
> 'Must still believe, for still we hope
> That in a world of larger scope
> What here is faithfully begun,
> Will be completed, not undone.'

And so we continue to look, and look wistfully to that
other possible illusion, that shadowy land of promise,
that far-away country—the Arcadia of the blest, where
there will be no worry, no abominable damps, and fogs,
and sudden changes of atmosphere, and no bores, and
perhaps no Philistines ; and where, at any rate, the

Bohemian and the Philistine will lie down peaceably
•together, and the lamb will not necessarily lie down
inside the lion.

> 'Now, alas, the poor sprite is
> Imprisoned for some fault of his
> In a body like a grave—
> From you he only dares to crave
> For his service and his sorrow
> A smile to-day.'

PHILISTINES AND BOHEMIANS.

Pope said of Dryden that 'he was not a genteel
man,—he was intimate with none but poetical men ;'
and it is recorded that Prior, after spending the
evening with Oxford, Bolingbroke, Pope, and Swift,
before he went to bed, would go off and smoke
a pipe, and drink a bottle of ale with a common
soldier and his wife in Long Acre. This is given as a
proof of his propensity for sordid converse ; however,
before we condemn Prior, we ought to know something of the scope of the soldier's social gifts.

I was sitting at the *Travellers'* with an old acquaintance, and I chanced to say that the *Athenæum*, next
door, was 'an excellent club, the best club in London,'
and I noticed my friend looked inquiringly-surprised;
so I backed my assertion with, 'Yes, you meet such
interesting people there ; walk in at 5 o'clock, of any
afternoon, and if you want information on Politics

or Art, Science or Literature, there you have
the first men in England to give it you.' ' Ah,' said•
my friend, ' it's all very well if one wants to meet
those sorts of fellows, but, you see, one doesn't want
to meet 'em.'

Prior's old soldier would have been quite thrown
away on my worthy friend, who, I fancy, must be what
is called a *Philistine*.

LIFE.

' When I consider life, 'tis all a cheat ;
Yet fool'd with hope men favour the deceit ;
Trust on ; and think to-morrow will repay—
To-morrow's falser than the former day ;
Lies on ; and while it says, we shall be bless'd
With some new joys, cuts off what we possess'd.
Strange cozenage ! none would live past years again,
Yet all hope pleasure in what yet remain ;
And from the dregs of life think to receive
What the first sprightly running would not give.
I'm tired with waiting for this chymic gold,
Which fools us young, and beggars us when old.'

John Dryden (1631–1701).

THE FIRST REAL GENTLEMAN.

'There have been persons who, being sceptics as
to the divine mission of Christ, have taken an un-
accountable prejudice to His doctrines, and have been
disposed to deny the merit of His character, but this
was not the feeling of the great men in the age of
Elizabeth (whatever might be their belief). One of
them says of Him, with a boldness equal to its piety,

> " The best of men
> That e'er wore earth about him, was a sufferer ;
> - A soft, meek, patient, humble, tranquil spirit ;
> The first true gentleman that ever breathed."

'This was old honest Decker, and the lines ought
to embalm his memory to every one who has a sense
either of religion, or philosophy, or humanity, or true
genius.' William Hazlitt.

THE CHRISTIAN RELIGION.

'The internal evidence of the Christian religion is
greater than the external. In the matter of external
evidence, other religions compete with the Christian ;
but in purity, wisdom, and power of cleansing the
human heart, it is alike original and supreme ; one of
its greatest characteristics is its opposition to the
monster vices of humanity.' Sir Philip Francis (1740–1818).

THE OLD STOIC.

'Riches I hold in light esteem,
    And love I laugh to scorn ;
And lust of fame was but a dream
    That vanished with the morn :

'And if I pray, the only prayer
    That moves my lips for me
Is, " Leave the heart that now I bear, ·
    And give me liberty ! "

'Yes, as my swift days near their goal,
    'Tis all that I implore ;
In life and death, a chainless soul,
    With courage to endure.'

                    Emily Brontë (1818-1848).

ARCHDEACON PALEY A JESTER.

Archdeacon Paley, seated at dinner, and annoyed by a draught of air, called out 'Shut this window behind me, and open that lower down, behind one of the curates.' This anecdote might have been told of the Rev. Sydney Smith. The clergy, when they condescend to jest, have a great advantage over the laity.

WITH A BOOK OF SMALL SKETCHES.

In days gone by, and year by year
I gleaned the sketchlets garner'd here :
Some pains they cost me, much shoe leather,
Before they all were got together.
Dear Children, I must flit anon ;
O guard them kindly when I'm gone.　　. F. L.

———◦◦◦———

A MOTTO FOR A PAPER-KNIFE.

Avia Pieridum peragro loca nullius ante trita solo.

Lucretius.

———◦◦◦———

AN EXCUSE FOR DRINKING.

'He who makes a beast of himself gets rid of the
pain of being a man.'　　Samuel Johnson.

FIVE MORE EXCUSES.

Good wine, a friend, or being dry,
Or lest we should be, bye and bye—
Or any other reason why.

An American had three reasons for not drinking,
and one of them a cogent one :—　.

1.—'I can't drink, for I've just lost a near relative.'

2.—(when he was much pressed) 'No, I really can't, you know—I'm president of a teetotal society.'

3.—(when he was much more pressed) 'No, I can't indeed—I'm liquor'd up to the bung.'

A LETTER OF HENRY FIELDING.

'On board the Queen of Portugal, Richard Veal, at anchor on the Mother Bank, off Ryde. To the care of the Post-master of Portsmouth—This is my date and y^r direction.

July 12 (?), 1754.

'Dear Jack,—After receiving that agreeable 10l. (?) from Messrs. Fielding and Co., we weighed on Monday morning, and sailed from Deal to the Westward. Four Days long but inconceivably pleasant Passage brought us yesterday to an anchor on the Mother Bank, at the Back of the Isle of Wight, where we had last night in Safety the Pleasure of hearing the Winds roar over our heads in as violent a Tempest as I have known, and where my only Consideration were the Fears which must possess any Friend of ours (if there is happily any such) who really makes our Well being the Object of his Concern ; especially if such Friend should be totally inexperienced in Sea affairs. I therefore beg that on the Day you receive this Mrs. Daniel

may know that we are just risen from Breakfast in
Health and Spirits this twelfth Instant at nine in the
morning.

'Our Voyage hath proved fruitful in adventures,
all which being to be written in the Book, you must
postpone y^r Curiosity. As the Incidents which fall
under your Cognizance will possibly be consigned to
oblivion, do give them to us as they pass. Tell your
Neighbour I am much obliged to him for recommend-
ing me to the Care of a most able and experienced
Seaman, to whom other Captains seem to pay such
Deference that they attend and watch his Motions,
and think themselves only safe when they act under
his Direction and Example. Our Ship in Truth seems
to give Laws on the Water with as much Authority
and Superiority as you Dispense Laws to the Public
and Examples to your Brethren in Commission.
Please to direct y^r answer to me on Board as in the
Date, if gone to be returned, and then send it by the
Post and Pacquet to Lisbon to

'Y^r affectionate Brother,

'H. FIELDING.

'To John Fielding Esq., at his House in Bow.
Street, Covent Garden, London.'

.*. I believe autograph letters of Henry Fielding
are very rarely met with. The above is in very good
preservation.

SONNET.

'When Letty had scarce passed her third glad year,
And her young, artless words began to flow,
One day we gave the child a coloured sphere
Of the wide earth, that she might mark and know
By tint and outline all its sea and land.
She patted all the world; old empires peeped
Between her baby fingers; her soft hand
Was welcome at all frontiers; how she leaped,
And laughed, and prattled in her pride of bliss!
But when we turned her sweet, unlearnèd eye
On our own isle, she raised a joyous cry,
" Oh yes ! I see it,—Letty's home is there ! "
And while she hid all England with a kiss,
Bright over Europe fell her golden hair.'

Rev. Charles Tennyson Turner.

———◦◦◦—

THE TOUCAN.

(REVIEW OF WATERTON'S 'WANDERINGS.')

How astonishing are the freaks and fancies of
nature ! To what purpose, we say, is a bird placed
in the woods of Cayenne, with a bill a yard long,
making a noise like a puppy-dog, and laying eggs in
hollow trees ? To be sure the toucan might retort,
To what purpose were gentlemen in Bond Street

created ? To what purpose were certain members of Parliament created ? pestering the House of Commons with · their ignorance and folly, and impeding the business of the country ? There is no end to such questions. So we will not enter into the metaphysics of the toucan.'   Sydney Smith (1769-1845).

———————

PRAYER.

'For so have I seen a lark rising from his bed of grass, and soaring upwards, singing as he rises, and hoping to get to heaven, and climb above the clouds; but the poor bird was beaten back by the loud sighings of an Eastern wind, and his motion made irregular and inconstant, descending more at every breath of the tempest, than it could recover by the libration, and frequent weighing of its wings, till the little creature was forced to sit down and pant, and stay' till the storm was over, and then it made a prosperous flight, and did rise and sing as if it had learnt music and motion of an angel as he passed sometimes thro' the air about his ministries here below. So is the prayer of a good man.'   Jeremy Taylor (1613-166).

———————

THERE IS A SEASON FOR EVERYTHING.

A good woman, in conversation with her pastor, was inveighing against the self-indulgence and pro-

digality of some neighbours, whom she prophesied
would come to grief in consequence. 'Such extrava-
gance, Sir,' said she ; 'they deny themselves nothing—
butter'd toast, *in season and out of season.*'

———•◇•———

FIRE.

'Sweet maiden, for so calm a life
    Too bitter seem'd thine end ;
But thou had'st won thee, ere that strife,
    A more than earthly Friend.

'We miss thee in thy place at school,
    And on thine homeward way,
Where violets by the reedy pool
    . Peep out so shyly gay :

'Where thou, a true and gentle guide,
    Would'st lead thy little band,
With all an elder sister's pride,
    And rule with eye and hand.

And if *we* miss, O, who may speak
    What thoughts are hovering round
The pallet where thy fresh young cheek
    Its evening slumber found?

' How many a tearful longing look
    In silence seeks thee yet,
Where in its own familiar nook
    Thy fireside chair is set ?

' And oft when little voices dim
    Are feeling for the note
In chanted prayer, or psalm, or hymn,
    And wavering wildly float,

' Comes gushing o'er a sudden thought
    Of her who led the strain.
How oft such music home she brought—
    But ne'er shall bring again.

' O say not so ! The springtide air
    Is fraught with whisperings sweet ;
Who knows but heavenly carols there
    With ours may duly meet ?

' Who knows how near, each holy hour,
    The pure and childlike dead
May linger where, in shrine or bower,
    The mourner's prayer is said ?

' And He who will'd thy tender frame
    (O, stern yet sweet decree !)
Should wear the martyr's robe of flame,
    He hath prepared for thee

'A garland in that region bright
   Where infant spirits reign,
Tinged faintly with such golden light
   As crowns his martyr train.'

'Nay, doubt it not : his tokens sure
   Were round her death-bed shown :
The wasting pain might not endure,
   'Twas calm ere life had flown.

'E'en as we read of Saints of yore :
   Her heart and voice were free
To crave one quiet slumber more
   Upon her mother's knee.'

John Keble (1792-1866).

ANTICIPATION OF DEATH.

'People who have not long to live sometimes appear
aware of the fact before it is even suspected by those
about them, and this is because their living powers
have become weak, and their nerves have communi-
cated the intelligence to the brain.'

John Hunter (1728-1793).

DISRUPTION.

It is on record that, not a great many years ago, a
Free church-minister of Scotland introduced into his

pulpit devotions a petition that 'we may all be
baptized into the spirit of disruption.'

It was to such as he that Voltaire referred, when
he said that the uncharitably righteous, in heaven,
would have to be content with their own salvation ;
they could not expect to have the satisfaction of seeing
their friends condemned.

A JOKE.

'What is a modern poet's fate ?
To write his thoughts upon a slate—
The critic spits on what is done—
Gives it a *wipe*—and all is gone !'

Thomas Hood.

I showed these lines to a distinguished friend.
'That is a joke,' said he ; 'now I will write something
that is not a joke.

'A TRUTH.

'While he lives—the Owls !
When he's dead—the Ghouls ! ! '

AN AMERICAN IN LONDON.

Two or three years ago, having made the acquaintance of an interesting American who had just arrived

in London straight from the Far West, I took him to
the Tyburnian side of Hyde Park, to introduce him to
a distinguished friend, whom he was very desirous to
know.   Our visit over, as we walked away, he said to
me, 'Does not Mr. Blank's poetry sell very well?'
and I replied (not knowing anything about the matter),
'Oh, yes, remarkably well;' and then he said something
which showed me he thought my friend Blank must
be enormously rich; and well he might, for it turned
out afterwards that he had supposed the Crescent in
which Blank dwelt was all one house, that Blank
owned the whole of it, and that the canal and villas
in the immediate neighbourhood belonged to and
were on his estate.   After all it was natural enough
that he should think so, having, as it were, so lately
dropt from the skies.

THE PILGRIMS OF PALL MALL.

My little friend, so small, so neat,
Whom years ago I used to meet
                    In Pall Mall daily,
How cheerily you tript away
To work, it might have been to play,
                    You tript so gaily.

And Time trips too !   This moral means
You then were midway in the teens
                    That I was crowning ;

We never spoke, but when I smiled
At morn or eve, I know, dear child,
        You were not frowning.

Each morning that we met, I think
One sentiment us two did link,
        Not joy, nor sorrow ;
And then at eve, experience-taught,
Our hearts were lighter for the thought,—
        We meet to-morrow !

And you were poor, so poor ! and why ?
How kind to come, it was for my
        Especial grace meant !
Had you a chamber near the stars,—
A bird,—some treasured plants in jars
        About your casement ?

Often I wander up and down,
When morning bathes the silent town
        In dewy glory,
Perhaps, unwitting, I have heard
Your thrilling-toned canary-bird
        From that third story.

I've seen some change since last we met—
A patient little seamstress yet,
        On small wage striving;
Have you a Lilliputian spouse ?
And do you dwell in some doll's house ?—
        Is baby thriving ?

My heart grows chill !   Can soul like thine,
Weary of this dear World of mine,
                    Have loosed its fetter,
To find a world, whose promised bliss
Is better than the best of this ?—
                    And is it better?

Sometimes to Pall Mall I repair,
And see the damsels passing there ;
                    But if I try to . . .
To get one glance, they look discreet,
As tho' they'd some one else to meet :—
                    As have not *I* too?

Yet still I often think upon
Our many meetings, come and gone,
                    July—December !
Now let us make a tryst, and when,
Dear little soul, we meet again,
In some serener sphere, why then
                    Thy friend remember.

1856,

MANY YEARS AFTER.

•I saw some books exposed for sale—
Some dear, and some—drama and tale—
                    As dear as any :

A few, perhaps more orthodox
Or torn, were tumbled in a box —
        '*All these a penny.*'

I open'd one at hazard, but
Its leaves tho' soil'd were still uncut ;
        And yet before
I'd read a page, I felt indeed
A wish to cut that leaf, and read
        Some pages more.

A poet sang of what befel
When, years before, he'd paced Pall Mall :
        While walking thus —
A boy—he'd met a maiden. (Then
Fair women all were brave, and men
        Were virtuous.)

They oft had met, he wonder'd why ;
He praised her sprightly bearing, (I
        Believe he meant it :)
No word had pass'd, but if he smiled
Her eyes had seem'd to say (poor child !)
        '*I don't resent it.*'

And then this poet mused and grieved,
And spoke some kindly words, relieved
        By kindlier jest :
Then he, with sad, prophetic glance,
Bethought him she, ere then, perchance,
        Had found her rest.

Then I was minded how my Joy
Sometimes had told me of a boy
   With curly head— .
' You know,' she'd laugh—(she then was well !)
' I used to meet him in Pall Mall—
   Ere I was wed.'

And then, in fun, she'd vow, 'Good lack,
I'll go there now and fetch thee back
   At least a curl !'
She once was here, now she is gone!—
And so, you see, my wife was yon
   Bright little girl.

I am not one for shedding tears—
That boy's now dead, or bow'd with years—
   But see—*sometimes*
He'd thought of Her !—that made me weep ;
That's why I bought—and why I keep
   His book of rhymes.
1878.

THE TWO RACES OF MEN.

According to Charles Lamb there are two races of
men, the borrowers and the lenders.

' Your *borrowers* belong to the *great race.* What a
careless even deportment hath your borrower ! what
rosy gills ! what a beautiful reliance on Providence

doth he manifest, taking no more thought than lilies !
● What contempt for money—accounting it (yours and
mine especially) no better than dross ! Your borrower
makes use of his money while it· is yet fresh ; a good
part he drinks away, some he gives away, the rest he
throws away, literally tossing and hurling it violently
from him.'

' Ah,' says Charles Lamb, ' when I compare your
borrower with the companions with whom I have as-
sociated lately, I grudge the saving of a few idle ducats,
and regret that I am now fallen into the society of
lenders and *little* men.'

The versatile Richard B. Sheridan was of course
an illustrious example of the *great* race. He was for
ever borrowing and hurling money violently from him ;
and yet, considering the innumerable sources from
which he drew his supplies, it was remarkable, and
indeed a wonderful proof of his ability, that he somehow contrived to keep his treasury always empty.
When he heard the rumour that the lost ten tribes of
Israel had turned up he was immensely elated. ' What
luck ! ' said the light-hearted being, rubbing his hands
cheerily, ' I had well-nigh exhausted the patience of
the other two.'

'WHAT AILS HIM AT THE LASSIE?'

A friend tells me a funny little story of. Mrs. ——
(the grandmother of Colonel M——), who was shown a
picture of Joseph and Potiphar's wife, in which of course
the patriarch exhibited his usual desire to withdraw
himself from her society. Mrs. —— looked at it for
a little while, and then said, 'Eh, now, and what ails
him at the lassie?'

I am sorry I cannot give the lady's name, as the
story says so much for her naïve simplicity.

QUAKERS.

'Though I reverence the philanthropy of the Quakers,
I cannot but remember that if the taste of one of that
body could have been consulted at the Creation, what
a silent and drab-coloured Creation it would have been!
not a flower would have blossomed its gaieties, nor a
bird been permitted to sing.'

GREEK.

'The best Greek linguist now living does not understand Greek so well as a Grecian ploughman did, or a
Grecian milkmaid ; and, with respect to pronunciation
and idiom, not so well as the cow she milked.'

A. MIRACLE.

'The account of the whale swallowing Jonah, though a whale may have been large enough to do so, borders greatly on the marvellous; but it would have approached nearer to the just idea of a miracle if Jonah had swallowed the whale.'

Thomas Paine (1737-1809).

EPITAPH IN THE CATACOMBS.

.   .   .   .   .   .

'I was born sickly, poor, and mean,
A slave; no misery could screen
The holders of the pearl of price
From Cæsar's envy; therefore twice
I fought with beasts, and three times saw
My children suffer by his law.
At last my own release was earn'd;
I was sometime in being burned,
But, at the close, a hand came through
The fire above my head, and drew
My soul to Christ, whom now I see.
Sergius, a brother, writes for me
This testimony on the wall—
For me, I have forgot it all.'

Robert Browning

THE COMMON LOT.

An ecclesiastic who was preaching before Louis XIV., happened to say during his discourse, ‘Nous mourrons tous.’ Then, remembering himself, the poor fellow turned in the direction of his monarch, and humbly bowing, added ‘ presque tous.’

CHURCHING A ‘LADY.’

A clergyman was churching a lady of very distinguished rank, and in consequence modified the formula thus :—‘ God save this *lady* (woman) thy servant.’ His clerk was also equal to the emergency, for he added :—‘ Who putteth *her ladyship’s* trust in Thee.’

A PORTRAIT BY VANDYKE.

Mr. Hazlitt thus describes the portrait of Lady Venetia Digby, at Windsor : ‘ It is an allegorical composition, but what truth, what purity, what delicacy, in the execution ! You are introduced into the presence of a beautiful woman of quality, of a former age, and it would be next to impossible to perform an unbecoming action with that portrait hanging in the room. It has an air of nobility about it, a spirit of humanity within it. There is a dove-like innocence and softness about the eyes ; in the clear delicate complexion, health and sorrow contend for the mastery. The mouth is sweetness itself, the nose highly intelligent, and the forehead is one of clear spirited thought. But misfortune has touched all this grace and beauty, and left its canker there.'

———•◇•———

A WHIMSICAL INVERSION.

' If once a man indulges himself in murder, he very soon comes to think little of robbery ; and from robbery he comes next to drinking and sabbath-breaking, and there is but one step from that to incivility and procrastination.

' Once begin upon the downward path, you never know where you will stop. Many a man has dated his ruin from some murder or other that perhaps he thought little of at the time.'   Thomas de Quincey.

———•◇•———

DIVES AND LAZARUS.

A Scottish divine was preaching on the petition of Dives that Lazarus should dip his finger in water and cool his tongue, and he commenced his discourse as follows :—' This appeareantly rezonable, but under the succumstances tottally inadmissable request,' &c., &c.

AN OPIUM DREAM.

'Then suddenly would come a dream of a far different character, a tumultuous dream, commencing with a music such as now I often heard in sleep. Music of preparation and of awakening suspense ; the undulations of vast gathering tumults were like the opening of the Coronation Anthem, and like that, gave the feeling of a multitudinous movement, of infinite cavalcades filing off, and the tread of innumerable armies. The morning was come of a mighty day, a day of crisis, and of ultimate hope for human nature, then suffering mysterious eclipse, and labouring in some dread extremity. Somewhere, but I knew not where ; somehow, but I knew not how ; by some beings, but I knew not by whom, a battle, a strife, an agony was travelling through all its stages, was evolving itself, like the catastrophe of some mighty drama, with which my sympathy was the more insupportable from deepening confusion as to its local scene, its cause, its nature, and its indecipherable issue. I (as is usual in dreams, in which, by necessity, we make ourselves central to every movement) had the power, and yet had not the power to decide it. I had the power, if I could raise myself to will it, and yet again I had not the power, for the weight of twenty Atlantics was upon me, or the oppression of inexpiable guilt. "Deeper than ever plummet sounded," I lay inactive ; then, like a chorus, the passion deepened. Some greater interest was at stake, some mightier cause than ever yet the sword had pleaded, or trumpet had proclaimed. Then came sudden alarms, hurryings to and fro, trepidations of innumerable fugitives. I knew not whether from the good cause or the bad, darkness and lights, tempests, and human faces ; and at last, with the sense that all was lost, female forms, and the features that were worth all the world to me, and but a moment allowed, and clasped hands, with heart-breaking partings, and then everlasting farewells ; and with a sigh such as the caves of hell sighed, when the incestuous mother uttered the abhorred name of Death, the sound was reverberated, everlasting farewells ! and again, and yet again reverberated,—everlasting farewells !' Thomas De Quincey (1785-1859).

TENPENCE HALF-PENNY.

A tall, thin man had a fat wife and a crooked little daughter. George Selwyn remarked that the assembled family always made him think of 10½d.

AN ACCOMMODATING VISION.

In the ' Iter Subterraneum ' of Baron de Holberg (an imitation of ' Gulliver's Travels') there is a priest,

r.

whose appointment to some lucrative post depends on his believing the sun to be, triangular. In vain he looks, and looks through his telescope ; he cannot think it otherwise than round ; so another ecclesiastic, of more accommodating vision, gets the place. The unsuccessful candidate afterwards questions the successful one as to how it was possible he could think the sun to be triangular, for, as for him, let him gaze at it how or when he might, it always looked round. The only reply the other gave was—' Certainly, it must be confessed, that for a triangular body it is very round.'

VOLTAIRE.

Voltaire spoke highly of Haller, and then was told he was very magnanimous to do so, as Haller had spoken in quite a contrary way of him. ' Perhaps,' remarked Voltaire, reflectively, and after a pause— ' Perhaps we are both of us mistaken.' Much the same repartee was made long before.

Voltaire was one day listening to a dramatic author reading his comedy, and who said, ' Ici le chevalier rit,' and he exclaimed, ' Le chevalier est *bien* heureux.'

JOHNSON'S CLUB-ROOM.

' The club-room is before us, and the table, on which stands the omelet for Nugent, and the lemons for Johnson. There are assembled those heads which live for ever on the canvas of Reynolds. There are the spectacles of Burke, and the tall thin form of Langton ; the courtly sneer of Beauclerc, and the beaming smile of Garrick ; Gibbon tapping his snuff-box, and Sir Joshua with his trumpet in his ear. In the foreground is that strange figure which is as familiar to us as the figures of those among whom we have been brought up—the gigantic body, the huge, massy face, seamed with the scars of disease ; the brown coat, the black worsted stockings, the grey wig, with the scorched fore top ; the dirty hands, the nails bitten and pared to the quick. We see the eyes and nose moving with convulsive twitches, and we see the heavy form rolling ; we hear it puffing ; and then comes the "Why, sir !" and the "What then, sir ?" and the " No, sir !" and the "You don't see your way through the question, sir !"'   Lord Macaulay (1800-1859). ·

DR. JOHNSON'S FATHER.

Mr. Michael Johnson suffered from a weariness of life, an unconcern about those things which agitate the greater part of mankind, and a general sensation of gloomy wretchedness.

EDUCATION OF CHILDREN.

A lady (probably 'a fond, maternal ass') asked Johnson what subjects she should first teach her children. His reply was characteristic : 'It is no matter what you teach them first, any more than what leg you shall put into your breeches first, madam ; you may stand disputing which is best to put in first, but in the meantime your breech is cold.'

WOMEN PREACHING.

'Sir, a woman preaching is like a dog walking on his hind legs ; it is not done well, but you are surprised to find it done at all.'

Samuel Johnson (1709-1784).

SOCIAL RANK.

Boswell—' I consider distinction of rank to be of so much importance in civilised society, that if I were asked on the same day to dine with the greatest duke in England, and with the first man in Britain for genius, I should hesitate which to prefer.'

Johnson—' To be sure, sir, if you were to dine only once, and it were never to be known where you dined, you would choose rather to dine with the first man of genius ; but to gain most respect, you should dine with the first duke in England, for nine people in ten that you met with would have a higher opinion

of you for having dined with a duke, and the great
genius himself would receive you better because you
had, been with the great duke.'

*** In these days it is not impossible but that you
may meet the duke at the table of the genius.

RADICALS.

'Sir, your levellers wish to level *down* to themselves,
but they cannot bear levelling *up* to themselves.'

Samuel Johnson (1709–1784).

A NEW RELIGION.

Lepaux, of the French Directory, invented theo-
philanthropy, and had a great wish to impose it on
France, but found, spite of his passionate endeavours,
that he made little progress.   He sought the advice
and assistance of Talleyrand.   'I am not surprised,'
said Talleyrand, 'at the difficulty you experience ; it is
no easy matter to introduce a new religion ; but I will
tell you what you might, at any rate, try : I recommend
you to be crucified, and to rise again on the third day.'

A BAD TEMPER.

There was a good bishop whose brother, though
possessed of many estimable virtues, had one serious

fault ; he had a very hasty temper. He was an un-
married man. One day, when he had got into a great
passion about some trifle or other, the bishop, instead
of reproving him, merely said, ' Ah, brother, I cannot
help thinking you have done a great kindness to *one*
woman—the woman who might have been your wife.'

SOCIETY.

Lord Jeffrey says, speaking of the tone of good
society, ' It has that air of gaiety and playfulness in
which persons of high rank seem, from time immemorial, to have thought it necessary to array, not their
courtesy only, but their generosity and hostility. The
constraint experienced by those who have not been
accustomed to high society arises from a difficulty, or
sense of propriety, in adopting the unceremonious
indifference that reigns around. The polished rude-
ness, the easy unconcern which goes straight to the
point, without the ceremonies that formerly were
considered polite, and which still remain, in some
measure, in the middle classes.'

The author of ' Friends in Council ' says there is a
light, jesting, flippant tone of talking about things and
persons now very common in society (exceedingly
different from wit), which stifles good conversation and
gives a sense of general hostility, rather than socia-

bility ; just as if men came together chiefly for the
purpose of ridiculing their neighbours and talking
·slightingly of matters of great concern.

A TYRANNICAL CONGREGATION.

A .dignitary of the Greek Church ventured to
alter the form of his ritual, and the historian, who
relates the event, gravely remarks : ' And his congregation, *justly incensed,* tore their bishop to pieces.'

POOR HUMANITY.

' Man is a bubble . . . he is born in vanity and sin ;
he comes into the world like morning mushrooms,
soon thrusting up their heads unto the air, and con-
versing with their kindred of the same production, and
as soon they turn unto dust and forgetfulness ; some
of them without any other interest in the affairs of the
world, but that they made their parents a little glad,
and very sorrowful. Others ride longer in the storm,
it may be until seven years of vanity be expired, and
then, peradventure, the sun shines hot upon their heads,
and they fall into the shades below, into the cover of
death and darkness of the grave to hide them. But if
the bubble stands the shock of a bigger drop, and out-
lives the chances of a child, of a careless nurse, of

drowning in a pail of water, of being overlaid by a
sleepy servant, or such little accidents, then the
young man dances like a bubble, empty and gay, and
shines like a dove's neck, or the image of a rainbow,
which hath no substance, and whose very imagery and
colours are fantastical ; and so he dances out the
gaiety of his youth, and is all the while in a storm,
and endures, only because he is not knocked on the
head by a drop of bigger rain, or crushed by the
pressure of a load of indigested meat, or quenched by
the disorder of an ill-placed humour ; and to preserve
a man alive, in the midst of so many chances and
hostilities, is as great a miracle as to create him ; to
preserve him from rushing into nothing, as at first to
draw him up from nothing, were equally the issues of
an Almighty power.'   Jeremy Taylor.

. *HYMNS.* ·

Devotional verse is one of the oldest and most
natural forms of song, and it is met with wherever the
instinct for worship takes outward form.

The following is Lord Selborne's admirable definition of what a good hymn should be : ' It should have
simplicity, freshness, and reality of feeling ; a consistent
elevation of tone, and a rhythm easy and harmonious,
but not jingling or trivial. Its language may be
homely, but should not be slovenly or mean. Affecta-

tion or visible artifice is worse than excess of home-
liness : a hymn is easily spoiled by a single falsetto
note. Nor will the most exemplary soundness of
doctrine atone for doggrel, or redeem from failure a
prosaic didactic style.'

I believe a martial ode is understood to be one of
the most difficult forms of metrical composition, and I
suppose we might say the same of devotional poetry,
seeing how very few fine hymns we possess.

It is thus that Dr. Johnson accounts for the
difficulty: ' The paucity of its topics enforces perpetual
repetition, and the sanctity of the matter rejects the
ornaments of figurative diction. It is sufficient for
Dr. Watts to have done better than others what no
man has done well.' This is trenchant enough, but it
seems hardly adequate, and I think the reasons are
not far to seek.

A hymn ought to be simple, clear, and direct, and
we know that rapt devotional feeling is apt to be
tinged with mysticism, which, in itself, is opposed to
lucidity of expression. Then the literary and devotional element must be harmoniously blended and
balanced, and it must be neither prosaic nor ornate.
Unity of subject and purpose is also essential ; indeed,
many hymns lose themselves in generalities ; and, last
of all, it must be the perfection of form.

It is very difficult to write a good hymn, and it is
remarkable that even our best hymn writers, like

Charles Wesley, have seldom succeeded in producing
more than one specimen of first-rate excellence; his
' Wrestling Jacob,' as a poetic allegory, is perhaps the
most perfectly sustained work in all English hymnody.
, Then we have Toplady's 'Rock of Ages,' where the .
harmony of the emblems, incongruous in themselves,
is secured by the devotional fervour that welds them
together.   These are both powerful hymns.   Then
there is the Rev. H. F. Lyte's beautiful 'Abide.
with me,' which should be confined to its five best
stanzas ; and lastly, Dr. J. H. Newman's exquisite
' Lead, Kindly Light.' I do not know any expression in
English poetry more beautiful in its way than the turn
of the thought in the last half of the last stanza.

Most of John Keble's hymns are on a fairly high
level ; but the best of them are not equal to these I
have quoted.   Keble wants clearness and simplicity in
thought or diction, and usually in both.   This may
be said of even his best pieces, such as ' Morning ' and
' Evening.'   And it seems to me that the devotional
poetry of the present day, in spite of its lyric sweetness
and delicacy, lacks the vigour and exaltation of the
older hymns.

Among other admirable hymns are the Rev. H.
Twells' 'At Even when the Sun ;' Dr. Arthur Stanley's
' O Master, it is good to be upon the mountain here ; '
Dr. Watts' ' Fairest of all the Lights above,' and several
in Dr. Martineau's excellent ' Hymns of Praise,' such

as 'Let no tears to-day be shed,' and 'Come tread once more the path with song.'

What is it that gives a hymn its popularity? Is it merely the music to which it has been set? Let us hope not. Very few hymns reach the great heart of the people : some, like Dr. Watts's, endure for generations, and English mothers are now singing them to their children in the back-woods of America, on the Himalayas, and wherever English mothers find themselves. Other hymns, apparently as beautiful, die unrecognised. It is difficult to account for this.

Sternhold and Hopkins's old version was rendered into a metrical form direct from the Hebrew. The Scottish version was by an Englishman, Dr. Rous ; and now we have Lord Lorne's skilful and harmonious rendering. The 23rd Psalm is lovely in all its versions, no effort of man can stale it, or quench its exquisite beauty.

———◆———

PRUDERY.

I have read that some societies in America are so very prudish that they actually object to using the honest word *leg*. For instance, a girl calls in hot haste on the doctor to say that her sister had broken her '*limb*.' 'Which limb is it?' says the doctor. 'Oh, I—can't—tell—you—which—limb,' says the girl. 'But you must,' says the doctor. 'Oh, dear, I—can't—

P

indeed, sir,' says the girl. 'Hang it,' says the doctor, losing all patience, 'Is it the limb she threads her needle with?' 'No, sir,' says the girl, immensely relieved. 'It's the limb she wears her garter on.'

CYNICS.

The world has pretty well made up its mind that your Cynic, *pur et simple*, is an odious being, and that our most lovable fellow-creatures have not a tinge of cynicism in their composition. I grant this, and yet, if Diogenes can only supplement his pessimist nature with a certain amount of playfulness, a fair dash of sensibility, and a sufficiency of benevolence, he blossoms into very pleasant company indeed. Our friend T. (as a writer) was an illustrious instance of this, and perhaps it is this mixture that makes Warrington so agreeable, and, I may say, so very attractive. But the most delightful example of all did not live a thousand miles from the Bridge of Allan.

ELOQUENCE IS EASILY MARRED.

As my revered friend was very anxious that his sermon should be a success, he had taken more than ordinary pains over it. However, during its delivery he did not feel that he had that hold on his congregation which he desired and which he usually obtained. There was a disturbing force, although he could not tell where. When the sermon was over, and not till then, he discovered that during the whole time of its delivery one of his soft thin silk gloves had been reposing on the crown of his head.

It requires very little to distract the attention of a congregation. If the famous Dr. South were exhorting us, or our Canon at St. Paul's, or even St. Paul himself, their eloquence would be seriously impaired if a sparrow chanced to fly into the church.

TO HIS MISTRESS.

'There is none, oh none but you,
　　Who from me estrange the sight,
　　Whom mine eyes affect to view ;
　　And chain'd ears hear with delight.

Others' beauties others move :
　　In you I all the graces find ;
　　Such are the effects of love,
　　To make them happy that are kind.

'Women in frail beauty trust,
　　Only seem you kind to me !
　　Still be truly kind and just,
　　For that can't dissembled be.

'Dear, afford me then your sight,
   That, surveying all your looks,
Endless volumes I may write,
   And fill the world with envied books.

'Which, when after ages view,
   All shall wonder and despair,—
Women, to find a man so true,
   And men, a woman, half so fair !'

Robert, Earl of Essex (1567-1601).

GOLOSHES AND SWINE.

I am told that the Americans call their india-rubber goloshes their *gums*. A man would quite naturally say, ' My friend will be here directly ; he is only wiping his " gums," on the mat.'

The hogs in Illinois are, or used to be, so thin that it required two of them to cast a shadow.

WIT.

Heine says that wit in its isolation is worthless. Then only is wit tolerable, when it rests on an earnest basis ; ordinary wit is no more than a sneeze of the reason.

SWITZERLAND.

'Go out in the Spring-time among the meadows that slope from the shores of the Swiss lakes to the roots of their lower mountains. There, mingled with the taller gentians and the white narcissus, the grass grows deep and free, and, as you follow the winding mountain paths (beneath arching boughs, all veiled and dim with blossom, paths that for ever droop, and rise over the green banks, and mounds sweeping down in scented undulation, steep to the blue water, studded here and there with new-mown heaps, filling all the air with fainter sweetness), look up towards the higher hills, where the waves of everlasting green roll silently into their long inlets among the shadows of the pines.'   John Ruskin.

———◆◇◆———

REPARTEE.

The Duke of Clarence, when Lord High Admiral of England, went down to Portsmouth to inspect the naval establishment. The first person he met was his jolly old messmate and friend Captain Jack Towers. The Prince took him by the hand, and laughingly said, 'Why, Jack, my boy, they tell me you are the greatest blackguard in all Portsmouth!' 'Oh,' quoth Towers, 'I hope your Royal Highness has not come down here to deprive me of my character!'

BENEVOLENT TACT.

Louis XIV., or some such mighty potentate, held a Court, and, what was most unusual with him, he broke it up suddenly, even abruptly. He afterwards privately explained his reason for so doing. He had observed M. de,—— who was very poor, and for whom he had a considerable regard, pocket a handsome chronometer *repeating* watch ; it only wanted a few minutes to the hour, and he was afraid that M. de ——, would be discovered and disgraced, if he remained till the watch struck, so he decided to get rid of him as quickly as he could.

CALCULATION.

'Jedediah Buxton could multiply nine figures by nine, in his head. The only good thing I heard come of this man's singular faculty of memory was the following : A gentleman was mentioning his (Buxton's) having been sent up to London, from the place where he lived, to see Garrick act : when he returned to the country he was asked what he thought of the player and of the play. " Oh," said Buxton, " I do not know ; I only saw a little man strut about the stage, and repeat 7,956 words." We all laughed at this, but a person in the corner of the room, holding one hand to his forehead, and seeming mightily delighted, called out, " Ay,

indeed, and was he found to be correct?" This was
the supererogation of literal-matter-of-fact curiosity.
Buxton's counting the number of words was idle
enough, but here was a fellow who wanted someone
to count them over again, to see if he was correct.
" The force of dulness could no further go." '

William Hazlitt (1778-1830).

———⚬———

ST. TERESA.

' Since 'tis not to bee had at home,
Sheel travell to a martyrdome.
No home for her confesses shee,
But where shee may a martyr bee.
    Sheel to the Moores, and trade with them.
    For this unvalued Diadem,
    Shee offers them her dearest breath,
    With Christ's name in't, in change for death.
    Sheel bargain with them, and will give
    Them God, and teach them how to live
    In him, or if they this denye,
    For him sheel teach them how to dye.
    So shall shee leave amongst them sowne
    Her Lord's blood, or at least her own.
Farewell then all the world, adieu,
Teresa is no more for you :

Farewell all pleasures, sports and joyes,
Never till now esteemed toyes,
Farewell whatever deare may bee,
Mother's arms or father's knee.
Farewell house, and farewell home :
Shees for the Moores and martyrdome.'

> > . . . . .

Richard Crashaw (1650).

'*THE BROTHERS*.'

I have the original MS. of Wordsworth's 'The Brothers.' At line 98 of the first edition (1800) the following passage occurs :—

' By this the Priest, who down the field had come
Unseen by Leonard, at the church-yard gate
Stopped short, and thence at leisure, limb by limb
He scann'd him with a gay complacency.'

In my MS. it runs as follows :

By this the Priest, who down the field had come
Unseen by Leonard, at the church-yard gate
Stopped short, and prying through his natural eyes
As through two opera-glasses, limb by limb,' &c.

W. W's. second thoughts were best.

DICK STEELE.

Sir Richard Steele, in the 'Tatler,' No. 49, says of Lady Elizabeth Hastings : 'Though her mien carries much more invitation than command, to behold her is an immediate check to loose behaviour, and to love her is a liberal education.'

Mr. Thackeray observes that the name of Richard Steele ought to be dear to all women, as he was the first of our writers who really seemed to respect them as well as admire them. His wife appears to have been very pretty, but to have had a temper, and to have been as prudish as he was impassioned, irregular, and reckless. Thus he writes to her a month after their marriage :

'Oct. 16, 1707.

' Dearest being on earth,—Pardon me if you do not see me till eleven o'clock' (very late hours for those times !), 'having met a school-fellow from India, by whom I am to be informed on things this night which expressly concern your obedient husband,

'RICH. STEELE.'

And again on March 11, 1708-9 :

' Dear Prue,—I enclose five guineas; but cannot come home to dinner. Dear little woman, take care of thyself, and eat and drink cheerfully. Let my best periwig be put into the coach-box, and my new shoes, for it is a comfort to be well dressed in agreeable company.

'You are vital life to your obliged, affectionate husband,

'RICH. STEELE.'

Then :—

'Tennis-Court Coffee-House, May 5, 1708.

'Dear wife,—I hope I have done this day what will be pleasing to you : in the mean time I shall be this night at a baker's, one Leg, over against the Devil Tavern at Charing Cross. I shall be able to confront the fools' (his creditors !) 'who wish me uneasy.

'If the printer's boy be at home send him hither, and let Mrs. Todd send by the boy my night-gown, slippers, and clean linen ; you shall hear from me early in the morning.

'RICH. STEELE.'

Another :—

'Five in the evening, Sept. 19, 1708.

'Dear Prue,—I send you seven penny-worth of walnuts, at five a penny; which is the greatest proof I can give you, at present, of my being, with my whole heart,   'Yours,

'RICH. STEELE.

'P.S.   There are but twenty-nine walnuts.'

'Sept. 20, 1708.

'Dear Prue,—If a servant I sent you last night got to Hampton Court, you received twenty-nine walnuts and a letter from me. I enclose the "Gazette," and am, with all my soul, your passionate lover and faithful husband,

'RICH. STEELE.

'Since I wrote the above I have found half a hundred more of walnuts' (I suppose she was very fond of walnuts, and that he knew it) 'which I send herewith.

'Dear Prue,—I am a little in drink, but at all times your faithful servant,

'RICH. STEELE.'

Dozens of similar letters follow with occasional parcels of tea, walnuts, &c.

The following is dated April 7, 1710 :—

'I know no happiness in this life in any degree comparable to the pleasure I have in your person and society. I only beg of you to add to your other charms a fearfulness to see a man that loves you, in pain and uneasiness, to make me as happy as it is possible to be in this life. Rising a little in a morning and being disposed to a cheerfulness . . . . would not be amiss.'

In another he is found excusing his coming home, being invited out to supper, and says, 'Do not send after me, for I shall be ridiculous.'

THE TURNSTILE.

'Ah, sad wer'.we as we did peäce
The wold church road, wi' downcast feäce,
The while the bells, that mwoan'd so deep
Above our child, aleft asleep,
Wer now a-zingèn all alive
Wi' t'other bells to meäke the vive.
But up at woone pleäce we come by,
'Twer hard to keep woone's two eyes dry;
On steam-cliff road, 'ithin the drong,
Up where, as vo'k do pass along,
The turnèn-stile, a-païnted white,
Doo sheen by day, an' show by night.
Vor always there, as we did goo
To church, thik stile did let us drough,
Wi' spreadèn eärms, that wheel'd to guide
Us each, in turn, to t'other zide.
An' vu'st ov all the traïn he took
My wife, wi' winsome gaït and look :
An' then zent on my little maïd
A-skippèn onward overjäy'd
To reach ageän the pleäce o' pride,
Her comely mother's left han' zide.
An' then a-wheelèn roun', he took
On me, 'ithin his third white nook.
An' in the fourth, a shreäkèn wild,
He zent us on our giddy child.

But yesterday he guided slow
My downcast Jenny, vull o' woe,
An' then my little maïd in black,
A-walkèn softly on her track ;
An' after he'd a-turn'd ageän,
To let me goo along the leäne,
He had no little bwoy to vill
His last white eärms, an' they stood still.'

Rev. William Barnes.

---◆◇◆---

RETIREMENT.

' Here, even here, on Salisbury plain, with a few old
authors, I can manage to get through the summer or the
winter months, without ever knowing what it is to feel
ennui. They sit with me at breakfast, they walk out
with me before dinner. After a long walk through un-
frequented tracks, after starting the hare from the fern,
or hearing the wing of the raven rustling above my
head, or being greeted by the woodman's " stern good-
night," as he strikes into his narrow homeward path, I
can " take mine ease at mine inn," beside the blazing
hearth, and shake hands with Signor Orlando Frisco-
baldo, as the oldest acquaintance I have. Ben Jonson,
learned Chapman, Master Webster, and Master Hey-
wood are there, and, seated round, discourse the silent
hours away. Shakspeare is there himself, not in

Cibber's manager's coat. Spenser is hardly yet returned from a ramble through the woods, or is concealed behind a group of nymphs, fawns, and satyrs. Milton lies on the table as on an altar, never taken up or laid down without reverence. Lyly's "Endymion" sleeps with the moon that shines in at the window, and a breath of wind, stirring at a distance, seems a sigh from the tree under which he grew old. Faustus disputes in one corner of the room with fiendish faces, and reasons of divine astrology. Bellafront soothes Matheo. Vittoria triumphs over her judges, and old Chapman repeats one of the hymns of Homer in his own fine translation! I should have no objection to pass my life in this manner, out of the world, not thinking of it, or it of me, neither abused by my enemies, nor defended by my friends—careless of the future, but sometimes dreaming of the past, which might as well be forgotten.'

William Hazlitt.

THE ADVANTAGE OF EMPLOYING AN AMANUENSIS.

A pedantic author told Sydney Smith that his ideas flowed more easily, and that he altogether composed better, when he employed an amanuensis. 'But are you quite sure,' said Sydney Smith, 'that he always puts down what you tell him?'

CONSOLATION.

·Dean —— was seated in a railway-carriage with
a lady in deep mourning, when a roughish-looking
man got in, and sat opposite to her. He regarded her
long and curiously, and then said rather abruptly, ' In
trouble, marm?' 'Yes, sir.' ''Usband or parent,
marm?' 'Neither, sir.' 'Son or daughter, marm?'
'Son, sir.' 'Army or Navy, marm?' 'Navy, sir.'
'Killed in action or died from natural causes, marm?'
'Killed in action, sir.' 'Got his chest, marm? 'cos
you know you've a right to *that*, marm!' 'Yes, sir.'
''Appy about his soul, marm?' 'Yes, sir.' ' Well,
I guess if you've got his chest, marm, *and you had a
right to that*, and you're 'appy about his soul,—not so
much of a trial, marm.'

DIFFERENT NATIONS HAVE DIFFERENT MODES OF INSTRUCTION, &c.

' In Britain's Isle, as Heylin notes,
The ladies trip in petticoats ;
Which, for the honour of their nation,
They quit but on some great occasion.
There men in breeches clad you view,
They claim that garment as their due.

In Turkey the reverse appears—
Long coats the haughty husband wears,
And greets his wife with angry speeches
If she be seen without her breeches.

. . . : . .

I mentioned different ways of breeding :
Begin we in our children's reading.
To Master John, the *English* maid
A horn-book gives of ginger-bread.
And, that the child may learn the better,
As he can name, he eats the letter.
Proceeding thus, with vast delight,
He spells and gnaws from *left to right.*'

Matthew Prior.

** These extracts are very pleasant, get ' Alma,'
and read it, and you will find more delightful things
than these.

PRIDE.

Lord Nobs was at least an arrogant man. Long after
he had grown up he chanced to meet his old French
schoolmaster. ' Do you remember, monsieur, that you
once nearly had me flogged ?' ' Ah, milor,' was the
reply, ' that was the one flogging that you did always
want.'

VANITY.

The Duke de Levi, a ridiculous man, had a picture painted of the Virgin Mary, and himself taking off his hat to her, the Virgin saying (as appeared by a scroll out of her mouth), ' *Couvrez vous, mon cousin.*'

A FAITHFUL PAGE.

Nearly one hundred years ago, my grandfather, Captain William Locker, was at dinner, and a servant-boy, lately engaged, was handing him a tray of liqueurs, in different-sized glasses. Being in the middle of an anecdote to his neighbour, he mechanically held out his hand towards the tray, but, as people often do when they are thinking of something else, he did not take a glass. The boy thought he was hesitating which liqueur he would have, and, like a good fellow, wishing to help his master, he pointed to one particular glass, and whispered, ' That's the biggest, sir.'

POETIC AND PROSE DICTION.

Poetic diction is picturesque, it often eschews generic terms, such as *tree* or *flower*, and prefers to mention some particular tree or flower, as :

> 'And every shepherd tells his tale
> Under the *hawthorn* in the dale.'

Under 'some tree's shade' would have been less picturesque. In the same way, 'Go, lovely *rose*,' is far more fitted for poetry than 'Go, lovely flower.' The same for prose, when it is impassioned. We prefer 'Solomon in all his glory' to 'a glorious monarch ;' but why do we prefer 'an ancient mariner' to 'an elderly seaman' ?

In Shakspeare's Plays prose and poetry serve, as a rule, for distinct purposes. Prose is used in the dialogue between servants, and in jest, and in light conversation.

For instance, Falstaff always speaks in prose, even in scenes where the other characters speak verse. Casca speaks prose when Brutus and Cassius speak in verse. One remarkable instance, where prose *is* used instead of verse, is in the speech of Brutus to the populace, after the murder of Cæsar. Elsewhere Brutus always speaks verse, but, in addressing the people, he refuses to appeal to their feelings, and affects a studiously cold, and unimpassioned style. His speech serves, in this respect, as a useful foil to Antony's highly-impassioned harangue. But even in this studiously frigid speech it is noticeable how, as soon as the speaker begins to *appeal to the feelings* of the audience, he approaches metre, and finally falls into it.

'As Cæsar loved me,' &c.

A good deal of this is taken from that excellent book ' English for English People.'

———◇———

A TEST.

If you wish to judge of a man's character and nature, you have only to find out what he thinks laughable.

INDEX.

ABS

ABSENCE of mind, 105
  Accommodating vision, an, 199
Acton, Philip, 'The Semi-detachment' (poem), 22
'Addison, Mr. Joseph,' 36
Admirals swear, old, 164
Affair of the heart, an, 160
America, photographing down west in, 158
— settlers in, 158
American restaurants, 93
American tall-talking, 112
American in London, an, 187
— prudery, 209
— exaggeration, 212
Angel, my guardian, 47
Arnold, Mr. Matthew, Philistines, 173
— Mr. Edwin, 'À ma Future' (poem), 55
Art collectors, 136, 141
— critics, 140
Atalanta in Camden Town (poem), 72
Atheism, 109
Autographs, the Maid of Athens, 11
— Thomas Hood on, 110

BAPTISMAL difficulty, a, 157
  Barnes, Rev. William, 'The Turnstile' (poem), 220
Baronets, 162

BRO

Barrow, Rev. Dr. Isaac, on want of earnestness, 1
Beaumarchais (P. A. Caron de) *blâmé* by the Court, 14
Beddoes, Thomas L., 'Love's Last Message' (poem), 162
Behn, Aphra (song), 69
Benevolent tact of Louis XIV., 214
Bible, William Hazlitt on the, 8
— Michael Scott on the, 10
Black blood, 7
Blake, William, anecdote of, 82
— — 'The Songs of Innocence,' 82
Blamire, Susanna, 'Barley Broth' (poem), 88
Bohemians and Philistines, 175
Boots, The Tight (poem), 95
Bores, 113
Borrowers, 192
Bossuet, Bishop J. B., 'L'Enfer,' 58
Braxfield, Lord, anecdote of, 52
Bride, a suitable, 68
Bridegroom, an intractable, 147
— a tractable, 147
Brontë, Emily, 'Plead for Me' (poem), 118
— — The Old Stoic (poem), 178
Browne, William, 'What wight he loved' (poem), 65
Browning, Mrs. Elizabeth B. (sonnet), 11
— Mr. Robert, 'In the Catacombs' (poem), 195
— rhyme, 105

BUL

Bulls, 42
— Irish, 42
— Scottish, 42
Bully, the, 63
Bunyan, John, swearing, 167
Burnand, Mr. F. C., on Rhyme, 103
Burns, Robert, his ' Lament for Culloden,' 15
Byron, Lord, with reference to Edgar Poe, 13
— — ' The Maid of Athens,' 110

CABMAN, the lady and the, 148
Calculation, by Jedediah Buxton, 214
Campbell, Thomas, 69
Capital in the wrong place, 37
Carlyle, Mr. Thomas, the morals of the Nineteenth Century, 135
Carracci, Ludovico, his ' Susanna,' 28
Carroll, Lewis, ' Atalanta in Camden Town ' (poem), 72
Cellini, Benvenuto, and his grandfather, 26
Ceremonious, almost too, 10
Church, High and Low, 38
Churching a lady, 196
Clarence, the Duke of, and Jack Towers, 213
Clergyman, Australian's notion of a, 166
Coleridge, Samuel T., on genius, 43
— —, on ghosts, 98
— Hartley, to his proud kinswoman (poem), 102
Collectors, fine-art, 136, 141
Common lot, the, 196
Compromise, a, 29
Consolation, 223

EAR

Cowper, William, with reference to Edgar Poe, 12
— — his poetry, 39
Crashaw, Richard, Herbert's ' Temple ' (poem), 6
— — ' St. Teresa ' (poem), 215
Cretans liars ? are the, 37
Critics, Fine-art, 140
Cynics, 210

DAIRYMAID, a sympathetic, 71
Dangeau, Abbé de, on grammar, 170
Decker, Thomas, the first gentleman, 177
De Quincey, Thomas, a whimsical inversion, 197
— — an Opium Eater, 198
Dickens, Charles, on Bores, 114
Diction, poetic and prose, 226
Dilemma, a, 37
Disruption, a prayer for, 186
Distinction, a (poem), 97
Dives and Lazarus, 197
Dobson, Mr. Austin, a Love Letter (poem), 90
Dogmatic teaching, 23
Doo, Mr., 125
Doomsday Book in danger, 93
D'Orsay, Count Alfred, and Mr. Raikes, 122
Douglas, Marian (poem), 112
Drinking, excuses for, 179
— excuses for not, 179
Dryden, John, ' A Lover's Attentions ' (poem), 17
— — Theocritus, 26
— — What is Life ? 176

EARNESTNESS, Isaac Barrow on the want of, 1

ELG

Elginbrod, Epitaph on Martin (poem), 58
Eloquence is easily marred, 210
Essex, Earl of, to his mistress (poem), 211

FAIRY funeral, a, 80
Family prayers, 119
Few wants, a man of, 75
Fielding, Henry, letter from, 180
Fine-art collectors, 136, 141
— — critics, 140
Fox, Charles J., 55
Francis, Sir Philip, the Christian religion, 177
Frere, J. H., a Fable (poem), 132
Froude, Mr. J. A., Luther and his wife, 25
Fuller, Thomas, fools, 38
— — the good yeoman, 38
— — the wounded soldier, 39
— — a good wife, 87
— — on John Wyclif, 98
— — on a cripple, 118
— — bear-hunting, 149
— — epitaph on Denys Rolle (poem), 159
Funeral sermon, a, 100

GENIUS, S. T. Coleridge on, 43
Gibbon, Edward, on C. J. Fox, 55
Gilbert, Mr. W. S., on Rhyme, 103
Goldsmith, Oliver, with reference to Edgar Poe, 12
— — and Thomas Hood, 75
Grammar, an enthusiast in, 170
Greek, Thomas Paine on, 194
Greenlander's Heaven, the, 94
Grote, George, education of the mind, 92

HYM

Guardian Angel, my, 47
Gusto, 100

HAMERTON, Mr. Philip G., on a portrait by Velasquez, 117
Hannay, Mr. James, 'Mr. Joseph Addison,' 36
Happy retort, a, 94
Haydn, Francis Joseph, his grim humour, 171
Hazlitt, William, on the Bible, 8
— — the St. Peter Martyr, 27
— — description of Stonehenge, 27
— — on a picture of Susanna, 28
— — on gusto, 100
— — on Thomas Decker, 177
— — on a portrait by Vandyke, 196
— — story of Jedediah Buxton, 214
— — retirement, 221
Heart, an affair of the, 160
Heine, Heinrich, on wit, 212
Heirs, 158
Helps, Sir Arthur, on Society, 204
Herbert, George, his 'Temple,' 6
High or Low Church, 38
Holmes, Dr. Oliver W., 'The Last Leaf' (poem), 44
— — on Nature, 120
Hood, Thomas, and Oliver Goldsmith, 75
— — his comicality, 76
— — The Poet's Fate, 187
Hook, Theodore, 141
Hugo, M. Victor, 'Gastibelza (poem), 58
Humility, real, 147
Humour and wit, the Scots', 43
Hunter, John, anticipation of — Death, 186
Hymns, 206

IND

'INDIAN Garden, My,' 105
Ireland, a Murder in, 146
— the Climate in, 147

JEFFREY, Lord, on Society, 204
Jerrold, Douglas, 142
Johnson, Dr. Samuel, anecdotes, 200–203
— — on Hymns, 207
— Michael, 201
Jonson, Ben, on Bores, 114

KEBLE, Rev. John, 'Fire' (poem), 184
— — Hymns, 208
Kempis, Thomas à, infancy, 108
Kleist, C. E. von, the poet, 28

LAMB, Charles, on liars, 34
— — a lively cheese, 121
— — borrowers and lenders, 192
Landor, Walter S., 'Regret' (poem), 116
Lecky, Mr. William E. H., on public worship, 23
Leigh, Mr. H. S., 'My Love she is a Kitten,' 84
Lepaux, Monsieur, a New Religion, 203
Liars, 32
Life, 172, 176
Locke, John, innate ideas, 159
Locker, Captain William, a faithful page, 225
London Lyric, 'A Rhyme of One,' 29
— — 'A Rhyme of Less than One,' 30
— — 'The Pilgrims of Pall Mall,' 188
— — 'Many Years After,' 190

PAL

London Society from an American point of view, 119
Lorne, John, Marquis of, hymns, 209
Louis XIV., his benevolent tact, 214
Lowell, Mr. J. Russell, 'Within and Without' (poem), 15
Lucky number, a, 91
Luther, Martin, and his wife, 25
Lyte, Rev. H. F., Hymns, 208

MACAULAY, Thomas B. (Lord), on Dr. Johnson, 200
Marlow, Christopher, compared to Edgar Poe, 13
Marriage, 83
—with a deceased wife's sister, 135
Martineau, Rev. Dr. James, collection of hymns, 208
Marvell, Andrew, To his coy Mistress (poem), 40
Meredith, Mr. George (poem), 142
Metaphysics, Scottish, 107
Milesian humour, 102
Millennium in Inverness, the, 160
Miracle? what is a, 67
Miracle, a, 195
Morley, Lady, Quakers and Bluecoat Boys, 133

NEWMAN, Rev. Dr. John Henry, the style and spirit of the classic writers, 13
— — Hymns, 208
Noise, a strange, 157

PAINE, Thomas, 194
Paley, Archdeacon, a jester, 178
Palgrave, Mr. F. T., on William Cowper, 39

Lightning Source UK Ltd.
Milton Keynes UK
UKHW010859070223
416609UK00007B/1881